PASSION, POWER,
AND PURPOSE

PASSION, POWER, AND PURPOSE

Essays on the Art of Contemporary Preaching

Edited by Joseph Coleson

Presented by
Dept. of Education & the Ministry

wesleyan
publishing
house

Indianapolis, Indiana

Copyright © 2006 by Wesleyan Publishing House
Published by Wesleyan Publishing House
Indianapolis, Indiana 46250
Printed in the United States of America

ISBN-13: 978-0-89827-336-6
ISBN-10: 0-89827-336-6

To all,
men and women alike,
who have been,
are,
and will be
bearers of good news to Zion,
this volume is dedicated,
with love and affection.

CONTENTS

ACKNOWLEDGEMENTS

A great many people make important contributions, large and small, to the production of any book; this volume is no exception. "Thank you" is but a small token of our gratitude, but the authors do thank most heartily all those who have helped in crafting this labor of love, and bringing it to the light of day.

The Wesleyan Educational Council has been very generous in funding and supporting this and other projects. We thank them for this essential support. In addition we thank Kerry Kind, whose counsel and support have been crucial, especially in the early stages of the project.

From the beginning, Don Cady, Publisher, and Larry Wilson, Editorial Director, at Wesleyan Publishing House have been unstinting and enthusiastic in their support, and in their guidance of the work through the editorial and publishing processes; our deepest thanks to them.

As it happens, all the contributors are married. Individually and collectively, we thank our spouses and families for their support, their counsel, and their patience.

Would space allow, many more should be named: those who have taught and mentored us; those we have been privileged to teach and mentor, and thus to learn from, as well; many others, in many contexts—one and all, be assured you have our sincerest gratitude.

FOREWORD

—————— ❀ ——————

A nyone called and commissioned to preach God's "Good News," and concerned with doing it well, can gain new insights and strength for the task by engaging the essays in this new volume. Many contemporary books on preaching speak mainly to the "worship wars" which sometimes appear to threaten the centrality of the sermon in future Christian communities. Such conflicts often have been part of the experience of the church. Not long ago, lofty pulpit-stands testified to the importance of what was being done there. At other times, in other places, whether one should have a single central-pulpit or a pulpit and a separate lectern became a cause of contention within local churches and even across denominations.

Now, aided by the burgeoning revolutions in media and communications technology, we often have to decide which screen to watch, or whether to fix our attention on the person with the microphone, standing or walking across a commodious platform. We also may have the option of having the sermon come through to us where and when we will, on a cellular phone, for example—maybe even while we're sitting in the pew!

Where and how all this finally may end, and what will prevail, no one can tell. But the contributors to this volume are convinced that somewhere, and somehow, the preaching of the "Story" will continue to be the central event in the worship life and mission of the church.

A major concentration on personal preparation and involvement of the preacher gives this work much of its value. Whatever the future place and delivery of the sermon may be, attention to these concerns can make the word about the Word more meaningful and fruitful. As the writers will consistently indicate, it is this continual, personal, experiential, spiritual preparation of the preacher—through open dialog with the Word, with the preacher's own self, with the Christian community, and with the world—that gives integrity to the sermon.

The grace of God working through the Spirit's empowerment and guidance of men and women living authentic lives in all these arenas makes for a more complete understanding of what God wants to say in the moment of the sermon. Its worth takes priority over where or when or by what means the sermon may be communicated. A strong reliance on the unity and integrity of Scripture as the ultimate authority for all truth-claims and an insistence upon calling all of Scripture to the witness stand are also hallmarks of a consistent Wesleyanism.

The authors of this volume intentionally address these and other important issues from within an evangelical, Wesleyan tradition. However, the questions raised and the reasoned responses given here will help evangelical preachers of any tradition to proclaim a more authentic and effective Word. With fervor, I invite you into this volume; by God's grace, it can help you become a better preacher. It should be said, too, that the quality of this initial volume bodes well for others which are to follow in this series.

—Melvin E. Dieter

INTRODUCTION
The Act and Art of Preaching

Joseph Coleson

I t may be the best-kept secret of our frenetic, kinetic, media-saturated, attention-challenged age: Every Sunday morning—and in smaller numbers on not a few Saturday nights, Sunday nights, and special occasions—approximately one billion Christians slip into a sanctuary for a one- to three-hour experience, the highlight of which usually is a speech by one person. All the rest of us listen in more or less rapt attention. We call these speeches "sermons." Some are enthralling; many are mediocre or downright boring. But we keep coming back.

The act and the art of preaching have been practiced for at least three thousand years. We may label as a sermon the prophet Nathan's parable delivered to David after the King's adultery with Bathsheba. A part of a prophet's responsibilities in ancient Israel and Judah was preaching to the people, even preaching to the king on occasion, as Nathan had preached to David. Jesus' Sermon on the Mount, Peter's sermon on the Day of Pentecost, and Paul's address before Festus and Agrippa are three of the most significant sermons in the early history of the church.

The importance of preaching waxed and waned during the first millennium of the church's existence. With the launching of the Protestant Reformation, preaching again assumed a central role in the worship life of the church and has remained in the foreground of Protestant worship ever since. As just one example, John Wesley, the major founder of the Wesleyan movement, preached on as many as forty thousand occasions during his long lifetime.

Pastors who give up preaching will find within a week or two that they have given up pastoring as well. Even with the "worship wars" of the last two decades, a church service without preaching (sometimes Christmas and Easter excepted) would seem strange indeed, whether in a Protestant or a Roman Catholic church. We go to church; we expect to hear a sermon.

Preaching matters. The health of our beloved church depends on the quality of its pastors' instruction, inspiration, and leading of worship.

Sermon preparation matters. Quality is achieved by preachers dedicating themselves to the serious work of research, study, and practice.

The personal preparation of the preacher matters. Every preacher would fail miserably on any given Sunday without the continual renewing of the Holy Spirit's anointing.

This volume is the collective effort of thirteen experts on preaching who are convinced of the eternal importance of preaching in and for The Wesleyan Church and its sister denominations. We believe God can and should be in and with the preacher—in the preparation leading up to the sermon, in the preaching moment itself, and in the results of the sermon both in the preacher and in the listening congregation.

This is not another "how-to" book on the homiletic craft, though we hope you will learn something about how to improve your preaching. It is not a book on biblical exegesis or exposition, though we hope you will glean wisdom on how to be a better student of the Word. It is not a book on how to catch and hold people's interest, how to be relevant, or how to call for a response at the end of the sermon, though perhaps reading this book will increase your congregation's participation in your services.

Rather, this book is intended to help pastors consider afresh what preaching is and why they do it. We remind preachers that they are privileged to tell regularly the greatest story, which stands eternally. We remind them, too, that they can know this story with both intellectual and experiential confidence. We encourage preachers to dwell in the story from week to week to make them compelling tellers of the story, storytellers parishioners will look forward to hearing each week. We explore why God still uses this ancient medium so powerfully today, but almost always only when preachers pay the price in understanding, in preparation, and in the hour of the sermon's delivery.

At two or three points, some of the chapters may seem to be pushing opposing emphases—but only to show that preaching is a complex skill, requiring years of dedicated effort to master. Not only must preachers exegete the biblical text and their own person; they must exegete the congregation, the community, the culture, and the cosmos in which they live and minister. Preaching is intended to be transformative on many levels, and effective preachers continually increase their awareness and specific knowledge of these many interlocking communities in order to call the community of faith to faithful and appropriate witness to God. Preaching is a multifaceted endeavor. Both the big picture and the small details are important to the crafting and delivery of a good sermon, and both are next to useless unless God delivers the sermon through the preacher.

In putting our thoughts on the printed page, we have attempted to articulate the Wesleyan vision for preaching. May God use this book, in its parts and in the whole, to increase your own vision of good preaching, transforming you and your hearers to the glory of God, the edification of the saints, and the welcoming of new daughters and sons into God's forever family.

THE HOPE IS IN THE STORY

What It's All About

Joseph Coleson

And the One who sits upon the throne said,
"Behold! I make all things new."

—Revelation 21:5 (Author's translation)

A believer, in the scriptural sense, lives in eternity. . . . His view is not
any longer bounded by present things: No, nor by an earthly hemisphere;
though it were, as Milton speaks, "ten-fold the length of this terrene."

—John Wesley, Sermon LIV, "On Eternity"

I stood on the campus of Azusa Pacific University in the eastern sector of the Los Angeles Basin a number of years ago. It was a beautifully clear, soft, autumn day in Southern California—a Seminary Day at APU. Representing the seminary where I was currently teaching, I stood at my table on a central campus walkway, along with reps from a dozen other seminaries, hoping that hurrying juniors and seniors, especially, would stop for a moment to talk about the possibility of graduate theological education. During a lull in passing student traffic, I fell into conversation with the representative next to me. We discussed Old Testament for a while—since I am a professor on the subject and he was interested. He related to me a statement one of his Bible professors had made in class, "The hope is in the story, and the story is in the Book." I don't know whether the line was original with that professor, but I've never come across it again since that day. Neither have I forgotten it; it continues to grip me. For I am increasingly immersed in that grand story, that only story.

Sometime after that, my wife and I watched a made-for-television movie, an updated version of the Pollyanna story. In this version the local pastor for years had preached sermons based on Scripture portions selected by the town's irascible "boss" who controlled pretty much everything that happened in town. A few weeks after the arrival of the Pollyanna character, when she had stirred up the town with her naïve and sunny optimism, the pastor announced at a town meeting that because of the rising tensions in town, he had recently begun reading his Bible intensively and had discovered it contains several hundred of what he called "glad texts." Furthermore, he declared, he was going to preach on those glad texts one at a time until he had preached through all of them. He wasn't going to let the "boss" rob him or the town of their joy any longer.

Truly, the hope is in the story, and the story is in the Book. Let us preach the "glad texts," the *euangelion*, the good news of the gospel of Jesus Christ.

THE STORY

If we are impressed to preach the "glad texts," how are we to be sure they really do represent the main thrust of Scripture? After all, a great many passages of Scripture, all the way from Genesis to Revelation, do not seem to be very good news. Human sin is a big part of the story, as are God's messages of judgment to come if sinners do not repent.

Precisely here is the point of this plea to steep oneself in the Scripture, to become intimately familiar with the true shape of the meta-narrative of this, the greatest story ever told.

So what is the story?

God created a perfect universe, including a perfect earth. Upon this perfect earth God placed the crown of this earthly creation, the first human pair. They were created to live in dependence upon God and in equality with each other. God commissioned them to exercise stewardship dominion over this earth. Exercising God's great gift of procreation, they were to bring children into the world, raising them to love God and each other and to treat each other as equals under God.

Sin came through the first couple's rebellious disobedience. Following quickly upon that first sin, the man declared himself to be the fullness of the designation "human" and relegated the woman to the roles of baby-maker and domestic servant. All human relationships since that time have been poisoned to a greater or lesser degree by the desire to rule over others; that, coupled with the desire for independence from God, constitutes the root, core, and basis of sin.

God did not destroy His creation, though, nor did He despair. God began to put into operation the plan of redemption formulated from before the foundation of the world.

> O God, our help in ages past,
> Our hope for years to come,
> Our shelter from the stormy blast, And our eternal home.
>
> —Isaac Watts, *Psalm 90*

Eventually God called Abraham and Sarah to be the founders of the first family of faith. From them came the nation of Israel. Though Israel's response was halting and inconsistent, God raised out of Israelite stock the Redeemer, Israel's Messiah and the whole world's Savior.

Jesus, the Messiah and Savior, died to rescue us from sin, from alienation from God and each other, and from death. Convinced by the Resurrection and empowered by the outpouring of the Holy Spirit at Pentecost, the church began to form and replicate itself as that joyous company of the redeemed which is well-nigh irresistible to the serious seeker after God—when the church gets it right, that is, and when the Holy Spirit whispers love into the seeker's heart.

This company of the redeemed is on the great journey, the great adventure, together. We follow our Prince, our elder Brother, our Heavenly Lover, our perfect Shepherd—the metaphors are nearly inexhaustible. Years of experience in the company of our Hero grow our maturity and deepen our love of the story.

THE SERMON

A sermon is the medium to convey the story, not a dialectic between "law" and "gospel." Preaching is not so much about dictating moral standards as it is empowering others with the good news of the ever-springing, overflowing, everlasting, overgenerous love and grace of God.

The Hebrew phrase *shema et-hattorah*, based on Deuteronomy 6:4–9, though not found there in precisely that form, can be translated either "obey the law" or "listen to the instruction." The first is the traditional translation of the Hebrew verb *shema* in a context like this with the noun *torah* as its object. But the second is an equally valid translation of this verb with this object, both grammatically and syntactically.

> Joy to the world! the Lord is come; Let earth receive her King.
>
> Let ev'ry heart prepare Him room, and heav'n and nature sing.
>
> —Isaac Watts, *Psalm 98*

Am I saying we should not obey God's law? Of course not. We should. God is sovereign; we exist only by God's creative and sustaining will and power. However, in the relational terms the Bible intends and which Wesleyanism attempts to explicate, "obey the command" is at the same time too harsh and not far-reaching enough. Throughout history "obey" has thrown on the screen of the human mind and psyche primarily the image of a king of absolute power and of terrible mien (in the old sense). Objectively, this is an accurate picture of God's transcendence; but God's desire and plan is not to relate to us merely as a King to His citizens. God desires, with a passion that would infuse us with unquenchable hope and self-conscious amazement could we know it even in only its hundredth part, to welcome us as sons and daughters into the very palace of heaven itself.

Consider, then, the alternative translation: "listen to the instruction." Those who are only subjects of their sovereign may "obey the command" with perfect performance, to all outward appearances, yet still with resentment, anger, and even rebellion in the inward parts. Just as little children delight to listen to, to learn from, and to put into practice the instruction of their parents, so the sons and daughters of the King of kings learn to know—admittedly, in part upon this earthly sphere—the why's and wherefores, as well as the what, of their heavenly Father's perfect will. They buy into it wholly, as into the family enterprise which will benefit all family members as it grows more and more into the perfect *telos* envisioned by the Father from before the foundation of the first galaxy or solar system.

God's instruction, then, is not the sum of all the harsh, arbitrary decrees of an unfeeling or cruel tyrant nor even the sensible but impersonal legislation of a benign but stern autocrat. It is the loving expression of the Father/Mother heart of God who passionately desires that everything good, and nothing of evil, befall us and be nurtured within us. God's instruction is always of grace, always of lovingkindness, always tending to our good as well as to God's glory. Rightly understood and applied, law is not opposed to grace. It is grace.

Slaves and sons alike may muck out stables and plow dusty fields. Domestic servants and daughters alike may scrub pots, and pans, and floors. Heirs are not exempt from hard work or danger. In fact, they should be the first to each. But slaves sleep in outbuildings, or in lofts, or even on the cold, hard ground. Domestics sleep in the highest attic or below stairs, stifling in summer, freezing in winter. Daughters and sons come in from hard work and danger to feast at the banquet table from the best china, the best cutlery, the best crystal, then to sleep in the palace on carved bedsteads under the finest linens.

Slaves and servants "obey the command," if we want to phrase it that way. But how much better to be daughters and sons, to "listen to the instruction" of our heavenly Father, of our heroic Elder Brother, and of our Divine Tutor and feast at our Father's table, ever in God's own presence.

Not every sermon can be, in and of itself, a "glad text." However, at a minimum, these understandings always should be the backdrop against which we preach. We who are undershepherds need to keep ever in mind the scriptural characterization of Jesus as He endured crucifixion; "for the *joy* set before him [He] endured the cross, *scorning* its shame" (Hebrews 12:2). Whatever the *explicit* agenda of any sermon, the *implicit* and intrinsic agenda of every sermon is to stir the deepest longing, resident in every human, to enter or to go more deeply into the story. Ultimately, going "more deeply" means getting better acquainted with the story's Author.

THE AUTHOR

We can preach with such freedom because we know the One who wrote the story. In the Old Testament, the character of God is profiled for us in the multiplied occurrences of the description of God as the God of *hesed* and '*emet*. *Hesed* means "lovingkindness"—love and kindness in thought, intention, attitude, word, and action. (Some define *hesed* as "covenant loyalty." "Covenant loyalty" certainly is included within God's *hesed*, but it barely begins to express the width, breadth, height, and depth of God's *hesed* toward us.) Think again of the ever-springing, overflowing, everlasting, overgenerous love and grace of God, and you will begin to get the first glimpse, the first delicious taste, of God's *hesed*, which is for you as surely as for anyone.

God's *hesed* would not mean much if it were either temporary or unreliable, switched on and off according to God's mood—assuming momentarily for the sake of the picture that God would have good and bad moods as we do. This is

> When I can read my title clear To mansions in the skies, I'll bid farewell to every tear, And wipe my weeping eyes.
>
> —Isaac Watts, *Hymns and Spiritual Songs, Hymn 65*

where the assurance of God's *'emet* comes in. *'Emet* means faithfulness, reliability. In the nature and character of God, God's *'emet* is eternal, everlasting, absolutely incapable of change or diminution. Since God's faithfulness cannot cease, falter, or waver neither can God's lovingkindness.

God's *hesed* and *'emet*, His eternally faithful lovingkindness, are our guarantee that the gospel of the Kingdom always has been, is, and always will be good news for any and all who will receive it. Nothing is more certain, because God's faithful lovingkindness is rooted in the very holiness and integrity of God, in God's nature and character, in who God is. If God ceased to be the God of eternally faithful lovingkindness, God would cease to be God, and we, at least, would cease to exist.

GLAD TEXTS

In Christian canonical terms, the good news begins with the first words of Genesis, "In the beginning, God created," and concludes with the last verse of the Revelation, "The grace of the Lord Jesus be with all." God's Word is the one Book worth making our own and the one story worth learning how to preach with joy, with verve, with gladness.

The story grows our anticipation of entering into His presence and seeing face-to-face the One we have adored from afar all these years:

Then Yahweh of Hosts will prepare for all the peoples on this mountain, a feast of fat things, a banquet of fine wines, choice cuts cooked in their marrow, fine wines aged on the lees. And on this mountain He will swallow up the covering that covers all the peoples, even the veil that veils all the nations. He will swallow up death for all time, and Lord Yahweh will wipe the tear from upon every face. And he will remove the reproach of His people from upon all the earth. For Yahweh has spoken (Isa. 25:6–8, author's translation).

It makes our hope sure, and our joy continues to grow as we near our heavenly destination:

Ho, everyone who is thirsty, come to the water. Even you who have no money, come, buy, and eat. Even come; buy without silver, and without cost, wine and milk. Why do you spend silver for what is not food, and your wages for what does not fill you up? Listen! O listen carefully to Me, and eat what is good, and delight yourself in abundance! (Isa. 55:1–2, author's translation).

It encourages us with the words of our Lord himself:

Take My yoke upon you, and learn of Me, for I am gentle and humble in heart; and you shall find rest for your souls. For My yoke is pleasant, and My burden is easy to bear (Matt. 11:29–30, author's translation).

It gives us a privileged look into the reality that will follow the passing away of time:

> And He showed me a river of the water of life, clear as crystal, coming from the throne of God and of the Lamb. In the middle of its street, and on either side of the river was the tree of life, bearing twelve crops of fruit, yielding its fruit every month. And the leaves of the tree were for the healing of the nations (Rev. 22:1–2, author's translation).

THE PREACHER

If we had to choose a text on bearing good news, it could well be two occurrences, or two versions, of the same declaration by Isaiah. The first occurrence is Isaiah 40:9: "Upon a high mountain get you up, O bearer-of-glad-tidings Zion! Raise your voice in strength, O bearer-of-glad-tidings Jerusalem! Lift [it] up! Do not fear! Say to the cities of Judah, 'Behold! Here is your God!'" (author's translation).

The other passage is Isaiah 52:7: "How lovely on the mountains are the feet of the bringer-of-glad-tidings, the one who announces 'Shalom'; the bringer-of-glad-tidings of good, the one who proclaims, 'Deliverance'; the one who says to Zion, 'Your God reigns!'" (author's translation).

> The term is over: the holidays have begun. The dream is ended: this is the morning.
>
> —Aslan, in C. S. Lewis, *The Last Battle*

Clearly God deems the bringing of glad tidings to be of utmost importance. The Hebrew language includes a verb dedicated solely to the idea of bringing glad tidings; Isaiah used that verb twice in each of these two verses. The preacher of this good news is important as well. The "bringer-of-glad-tidings" is a singular participial form in Hebrew.

The gender of this preacher, however, doesn't seem to matter at all. In Isaiah 40:9 the two participles are feminine singular whereas in 52:7 both are masculine. Notice that the two feminine occurrences take canonical precedence over the two masculine occurrences. I have a hunch that Isaiah (we may read "God" here) did not want any exegetes through the ages to think women were unfit agents to be "bringers-of-glad-tidings" nor that having women fulfill this joyous mission is somehow an afterthought in the mind of God. Do I speculate too much on that point? Never mind. If you are female, you are privileged to be a *mevasseret*, a bringer-of-glad-tidings. If you are male, you are privileged to be a *mevasser*, a bringer-of-glad-tidings. (I put those two statements in Isaiah's order, rather than presuming to rearrange the prophet.) God's design, God's desire, God's delight is to privilege, equip, and empower persons of both genders to bring the life-saving, life-engendering, life-expanding glad tidings of God's peace, love, and joy to all persons of every people group.

> It is only in following the Christ who was raised from suffering, from a god-forsaken death and from the grave that [faith] gains an open prospect in which there is nothing more to oppress us, a view of the realm of freedom and of joy.
>
> —Jürgen Moltmann, *Theology of Hope*

More importantly, the preacher must experience the Scripture for him or herself. The preacher is privileged to learn to revel in it as the good news, joyous proclamation, great adventure and, yes, sweet seduction of our Heavenly Lover and Bridegroom. All this must become the rich experience of the preacher before it can reach the congregation. We must live in the text before we can invite the congregation into it. We must experience on a daily basis the truth of the sidewalk adage, "The Hope is in the story, and the story is in the

Book." *We* must come to know spiritually, cognitively, and emotionally—in every way—that by God's grace we do belong in the story.

THE AUDIENCE

One critical reason we must give ourselves without reservation to bringing glad texts to our hearers is because the average Western hearer, saint or sinner, no longer perceives God's message as good news. The average non-Western hearer either has never heard the gospel or has not heard it so as to perceive it as good news.

Let me explain. When I was growing up in the United States in the 1950s and '60s, we still were, for all practical purposes, a monolithic culture. By way of illustration, John F. Kennedy lost the 1960 national presidential election by a narrow enough margin that his loss could be attributed to the conservative Protestant anti-Catholic, anti-Vatican vote. (Kennedy took office in January, 1961, because Richard Nixon decided not to contest the election in at least two states which were stolen for Kennedy by fraudulent vote counts. Even die-hard politicos who were around then will concede that now. I've heard them do so on national television.)

The old Protestant monolith in the U.S. is shattered now—for all the good and all the ill that entails—as it is in all countries formerly dominated by the heirs of the Reformation. Similarly, formerly Catholic and Orthodox countries are no longer monolithically Catholic or Orthodox. In no formerly Christian nation or people group dare we now assume a massively pre-evangelized population.

The number-one practical implication from the shattering of the monolith, for our purposes here, is that we must assume people have *no* background or experience in hearing the gospel of Jesus Christ as good news. If they are old enough to have heard it when Christianity in any of its forms was the dominant religious category, they almost certainly will remember hearing it not as good news but as a guilt-inducing damper on fun or as a legalistic, hypocritical fraud—very likely, as both. I know that sounds harsh, but I could cite chapter and verse in case after case of friends, acquaintances, and those I've merely read about from my own baby-boomer generation. It's at once a shame and a heartbreak.

On the other hand, those who are not old enough to have grown up in a culturally Christian environment, or who are from a traditionally non-Christian location or people group, may not have heard the good news of Christ at all. If they have heard, they likely had it delivered in that same legalistic and either guilt-inducing or hypocritical mode, as well. Furthermore, for many astute non-Westerners, the Bible has come across as but another tool in the service of the West's political, economic, and cultural imperialism, whether we messengers have intended that (as sometimes we have) or not.

Let's add the further complication of postmodernism heavily influencing especially the younger potential hearers of the good news in every part of the globe today. For many of them, we cannot begin either with sin and guilt or with the logical, linear reasoning process—both of which have been vastly popular weapons in the arsenal of Protestant Reformed-dominated apologetics and evangelism for much of the past five hundred years. The popularity of these strategies has waxed rather than waned in recent decades even as the bandwidth of their effectiveness has narrowed.

Today many young people, especially, are unimpressed by appeals to guilt as an inducement to accept the Christian faith. They don't begin with the knowledge that a God exists who cares about their moral conduct because He cares about them. As they hear the story wherein the hope lies, and as the Spirit woos them, they will come to that understanding. But it may well be a slow and cautious journey with fits and starts—even with detours, short or long.

Many young people are not impressed, either, by the rationalism which has characterized much of the Protestant reading and telling of the story. They may agree that two plus two equals four, but that fact is to them no compelling argument to change their ways. In addition, they may be perfectly content to accept also that two plus two equal five and see no need to decide between the two competing results precisely because they do not see them as competing. Banks and ATMs do not let us get away with that sort of math on the literal level of numbers; but in the realm of religious belief, such a hodgepodge of doctrinal systems, Christian and non-Christian alike, thoroughly stirred and simmered in a stew of multifarious origins, is today, in many quarters, rather the rule than the exception.

THE HOPE

Thanks be to God, Wesleyanism is relationally-oriented and relationally-driven. We know a hundred ways to be and speak and act so as to draw people to the Christ whose story we tell rather than try to blast them into it by the explosive power of our evangelistic weapons of mass deduction.

Please understand; I am not decrying logic *as* logic. As a biblical scholar, linguist, historian, and literary critic, I must use logic and reason and all they entail. They are some of my most important stocks in trade; I couldn't function without them. But logical reasoning is not the place to start with postmoderns, nor with people who have heard the story as bad news or as no news rather than as good news.

Neither am I suggesting that an understanding of sin and guilt and of how God has provided for our deliverance from them are trivial subjects. But shame rather than guilt has been and largely remains the most powerful negative motivator for much of the non-Western world. In the West, too, guilt has lost most of its power to motivate toward personal reform, and guilt is too individualistic to stand as the sole negative arbiter anyway. Assuaging individual guilt encourages a privatized faith, and a merely privatized faith runs counter to everything in the Judeo-Christian Canon.

Let me repeat: Wesleyanism is relationally-oriented and relationally-driven. If it were appropriate to begin with logical explanations of sin and guilt, we could do it with the best of our evangelistically-minded brothers and sisters. But those are not the beginning of our understanding of the story, nor are they—by quite a long measurement—the most important elements we understand the Book to be telling. To be true to our biblical understanding and to our Wesleyan heritage, viewed in their entirety, we must start with the simple telling of the Story, which is the presentation of God's passion for relationship with us and the lengths to which God has already gone to reestablish that primeval relationship through the successful quest of our divine Elder Brother and Hero, Jesus Christ. Let people experience and ponder the description of the monsters—sin, death, and hell—when they see them lying dead at His feet.

> Whatever Christ is and does serves as a preparation for the resurrection; it is a message of joy and an overture to happiness.
>
> —Bernard Haring,
> *Hope Is the Remedy*

Truly, the hope is in the story, and the story is in the Book. In eternal terms, its significance makes it the only narrative ever told. In literary terms, its happy ending makes it a comedy, not a tragedy. In terms of relevance, it offers all who encounter it the opportunity to become a part of it. In accepting that offer, every hearer's story becomes a story with a happy ending, too, with eternal significance. Only by refusing does the hearer guarantee that his or her own story will end tragically, apart from the God of all joy. We preachers, then, must interpret the story in ways that make it obvious to our hearers that it is, or can become, good news for them.

ACTION SUGGESTIONS

If you do not drink deeply and often from Scripture's life-giving waters already, let me ask you to consider just a few of many possible suggestions to get you started.

1. Carry the Bible in a convenient format and read it at odd times. The *New Living Translation* and Peterson's *The Message* are good for such reading. Start with familiar stories or with stories you know should be familiar but aren't. Read Ruth seven times, for pure enjoyment, before going on to Esther for the same reason. Read the Sermon on the Mount seven times, and don't forget to laugh at the ludicrous image of the man with the beam in his eye offering to take a speck of dust out of his neighbor's eye.

2. When you come across a passage that makes you laugh—or cry—for joy, print it out and put it in your pocket. Read it seven times a day for a week. Then see if you can memorize it; it should be easy by then.

3. Read the shorter psalms until you find one that makes you want to dance or sing for joy, or one that speaks to you in your sorrow, your doldrums, or even your depression. Carry a copy around and read it until you know it by heart.

4. After awhile, these texts will beg you to preach them. And you should begin to preach them. But spend the time required to craft your sermons well. In every sermon, your goal should be to do justice to the laughing, dancing, joyous text or to the sorrowful, disquieting text, if that's the one that has captured you. Whichever it may be on a given occasion, soon you will find yourself content to be listed forever among the vast and happy company of the privileged—the tellers of that great and only story.

FOR FURTHER READING

Easy-to-read Bibles like the *New Living Translation* and *The Message* are good for some of the reading suggested here. But don't neglect translations that follow more closely the "formal equivalence" paradigm, such as the *New Revised Standard Version.*

Anything by C. S. Lewis will help anyone to be a better preacher. That's a sweeping statement; but read Lewis awhile, and I think you'll agree.

Most of what Walter Brueggemann has produced is helpful and inspirational to and for the preacher, even though sometimes Brueggemann's interpretive paradigms are not especially attractive in the light of Wesleyan theology.

PREACHING
WITH POWER

Led by the Spirit

Joseph Dongell

It is the Spirit who gives life.
—John 6:63 (NASB)

The Spirit works to enable the faithful to hear
and respond to Christ's living personal presence.
—Thomas Oden, *Life in the Spirit*

Dennis Kinlaw tells of his experience as a young preacher when an elderly gentleman met him at the church door after the sermon. In an unusually direct but loving way, the senior offered this keen advice: "Son, this world doesn't need to hear what you think. What it needs to hear is what God thinks. Go home and get down on your knees with your Bible and stay there until you know what God thinks. And the next time you stand up to preach, tell the people what God thinks."[1]

In the late 1970s John R. W. Stott was contracted as primary preacher at an Urbana missions conference. True to his gifts and calling, Stott engaged in lengthy and intensive preparation for the series of sermons on Romans he planned to deliver. In the final climactic evening service, Stott stepped forward to the podium and delivered, without notes, the sermon he had so carefully crafted and memorized. The Holy Spirit was present in a mighty way, both extending and confirming calls of many to missionary service. After the service, as Stott was walking back across the university campus to his room, a young engaged couple who had heard the sermon recognized him and stopped him. "Oh, Dr. Stott!" they exclaimed. "What a powerful sermon! Thank you so much for saying exactly what we needed!" Stott replied, "Would you like a copy of the manuscript?" Immediately their faces fell in shocked disbelief. "Manuscript? But we thought *the Spirit* was speaking through you!"[2]

CRAFT AND MYSTERY

Walk through any well-stocked religious bookstore or theological library and you will find shelves bursting with books about the Holy Spirit on the one hand and about the art and craft of preaching on the other. Fewer writers have explored in any detail the *overlap* between these two topics crucial for the Christian preacher's life and ministry.

Even a few minutes of scanning will reveal that most books devoted to preaching focus on the *technique* of preaching: organizational approaches, sermon structure and development, style and diction, illustrations and vivid language, strategies of persuasion, and effective delivery. After all, most of us who preach are drawn like moths to the light by anything promising through "six easy steps" or "eight dynamite strategies" to transform us into compelling speakers. But the Spirit's presence in our preaching is not so easily defined by a checklist or a set of learned skills. The Spirit works at a deeper level, moves in mysterious ways, and follows a timetable other than our own. Who is able to speak definitively about matters like these?

That's not to say authors are not writing books about the Holy Spirit; they're just not writing about the Spirit working in the painstaking work of sermon preparation. Much contemporary teaching about the Holy Spirit gravitates toward one of three foci: a focus upon *expression*—rejoicing in "praise and worship"; a focus upon *gifts*—identifying and deploying spiritual gifts within the body of Christ; or a focus upon *personal growth*—owning the Spirit's role in the Christian's daily encounter with things like suffering, temptation, or decision-making. While attention to each of these has benefited the church in obvious ways, this same attention has an unrecognized downside. For like an actor successful in early films, the Holy Spirit has too often been typecast to fit only within these limited roles while other dimensions of the Spirit remain unknown and unexplored. Ironically, we may fervently preach *about* the Holy Spirit's ministry in the modes named above without considering how the Spirit moves *within the act of preaching itself.*

Perhaps authors dare not broach the topic of crafting a sermon in the Spirit because they are afraid they would have no readers. Attention to the Holy Spirit is fading fast in some circles with the rising tide of generic "God-talk." Christians are abandoning the Trinitarian language of Father, Son, and Holy Spirit, preferring instead to talk in reductionistic fashion about "what *God* is doing in your life" or "whether you love *God* with all your heart" or "what *God* might be saying to you now." In our contemporary impatience with doctrine of any kind, with language sounding like our grandparents', and with things not immediately practical, this generation may in effect be leading the Holy Spirit out to pasture for a gentle retirement. As one child reported, "I just pray to 'God,' and let them sort out their own mail up there."

SPIRIT-LED PREACHING

What a different world we meet in the apostolic church. Even a casual reading of Acts brings us face-to-face with an emerging Church whose preachers were cleansed, empowered, caught up, directed, and informed by the *Holy Spirit*.[3] This Spirit, as Jesus declared, was promised and then poured out upon the church by the *Father* (Luke 24:49; Acts 1:4). The New Testament writers were not engaged in complex theologizing about the inner workings of the Trinity, but they did reveal—in their prayer, preaching, and worship—how vibrantly aware they were of the *triune* God. They were able to speak of how Father, Son, and Spirit each participate in distinctive ways to lead the church in its life and mission.

If the story of the emerging church in Acts is saturated with references both to the Holy Spirit and to preaching, it will be fruitful to explore just how these two impinge on each other both in Acts and in the rest of Scripture.

When we open ourselves to preaching the *whole* of Scripture rather than strategically chosen passages, we invite the *full range* of the Holy Spirit's ministry among us: "All scripture is inspired by God and profitable for teaching, for reproof, for correction, for training in righteousness, so that the man of God may be adequate, equipped for every good work" (2 Tim. 3:16–17 NASB). If the Spirit has inspired all of Scripture, let us trust the whole of Scripture to supply the rich range of nutrients both we and our people need. Let us break through into a new willingness to let the Bible call the shots, set the agenda, and lead us in directions we haven't finely pre-engineered.

CHRISTOCENTRIC

We haven't declared the last word about the content of preaching, even if we have all agreed that it must be biblically focused or that it must embrace the whole of Scripture. After all, we Christians have come to confess and embrace *Christ Jesus* as the One through whom the Father created the world, through whom the Father redeems believers, and through whom the Father will judge the world. This means the Bible is not, in the final analysis, simply a collection of right doctrines or of reliable truths or of useful insights for better living. Above and beyond this, the Bible's parts and components combine to showcase the crucified and risen One as Lord of the Church and of the World. We have not seen the beauty and power of Scripture until we have seen Him as its glowing Center!

In the days after His resurrection, Jesus himself opened the eyes of His disciples to understand the Scripture to see how the law of Moses, the words of the prophets, and the Psalms all anticipated His incarnation, His death, His resurrection, and the world-wide proclamation of His gospel (Luke 24:44–47). The practices of the apostles and the early church show they "saw" Jesus in the Old Testament—not in narrow proofs from prophecy, but in the warp and woof of the whole. This does not require us to ignore the sense of God's Word as it addressed the particular circumstances of ancient Israel. It does mean, however, that we do not break over into *Christian* preaching until we also set the Word of God to Israel into its proper relationship to the Living Word, the Word made flesh. Put simply, all truly Christian preaching points clearly to Christ, the center of the Father's creating and redeeming work.

> The [c]hurch is not at the whim of the minister; he is not allowed to teach and preach as he alone wishes. No, [other leaders, too] . . . are given the responsibility for the right proclamation of the Word.
>
> —Donald Bruggink and Carl Droppers, *Christ and Architecture*

We are not required by this focus to reduce the entire business of the Church and of preaching to "evangelism." The logic behind this reduction at first glance seems inescapable: No one can make it to heaven without being saved; therefore, salvation is the greatest gift anyone can ever receive; therefore, evangelism must be the Church's highest goal. Scripture, however, embraces for the Church the larger, more demanding vision of *transformation*. Time and again, the driving passion expressed by Jesus and His apostles is not simply for conversion but for wholeness characterized by Christlikeness. Notice how the Great Commission includes within it Jesus' requirement that disciples be taught "to observe *all* that I commanded you" (Matt. 28:20 NASB, italics added). Evangelistic ventures that do not embrace with equal passion the shaping of our lives in obedience to Jesus have reduced the Great Commission to the "Great Sign-Up." J. R. Mitchell often captured this note in his preaching when he declared, "God loves us too much just to 'save us'; He aims for nothing less than to transform sinners into saints."[4] Sometimes we have focused on an initial showing of fruit, when Jesus appointed us to bear fruit that would *last* (John 15:16).

The seamless connection between "preaching Christ" and "preaching transformational holiness" is beautifully expressed by Paul to the Colossians in his mission statement: "We proclaim *Him* [Christ], admonishing every man and teaching every man with all wisdom, so that we may present every man *complete in Christ*" (Col. 1:28 NASB, italics added). Paul urged the Philippians to have the attitude of Christ, an attitude of humble obedience to God extending right into the very jaws of death (Phil. 2:5ff.). Our point is this: When we commit ourselves to preach Christ, we necessarily have committed ourselves to preach holiness, the life modeled after and transformed by the indwelling Christ. Here is the whole gospel and the comprehensive salvation we are called to proclaim.

Have we lost track of the Holy Spirit, now that we have centered our preaching upon Jesus the Living Word? Not at all, for in the

Gospel of John we find Jesus teaching His disciples about the special relationship between himself and the Holy Spirit. In the Upper Room Discourse (John 13–17), Jesus labored to calm the fears of His disciples who were learning that He would be taken from them by a violent death. To allay their fears of becoming "orphans" in His absence, Jesus assured them He would send them "another Comforter," another presence who would indwell the disciples *to represent Jesus himself* among them.

John's gospel consistently develops this theme. The Spirit's role is *not* to draw attention to the Spirit or to proclaim a new message beyond the message of Jesus. Rather, the distinctive role of the Spirit is to draw attention to Jesus, to focus all eyes upon the Risen Lord, and to bring to remembrance the words and mission of the Son. If we want to create an environment conducive to the presence and power of the Spirit among us, we must focus our energy on magnifying the Person and work of the Beloved Son. In short, Spirit-led preachers will be Christocentric preachers.

WELL-PLANNED

The best-laid preaching plans are not immune to derailment. The preacher steps forward, fully prepared to deliver the sermon, but at that very moment a strong inward impulse (of the Spirit) compels him or her to set the notes aside and venture in an unexpected direction. In these moments the Spirit proves that our orders of worship ought to be suggestions, not ironclad strictures eliminating the freedom of God to surprise us.

Some of us may value smoothness and professionalism to such a degree that we rule out anything having rough edges or uncertain outcomes. By treating worship services as productions that must follow seamless and calculated transitions, we may impress some audiences while suppressing the unscripted work of God. Paul's admonition to do church "decently and in order" (1 Cor. 14:40 RSV) cannot be reduced to a set of rules but must be spiritually discerned through constant attention by leaders and laypeople alike.

> The incarnation, preaching, and death of Jesus Christ were designed to represent, proclaim, and purchase for us this gift of the Spirit; and therefore says the Apostle, "The Lord is that Spirit," or *the* Spirit.
>
> —John Wesley, Sermon CXLI, "On the Holy Spirit"

At the same time, paradoxically, others of us often *overvalue* the spontaneous and unscripted, and unwisely assume that we hear the Spirit only or especially in moments of surprise. Some of us may have unwittingly absorbed the false theology that human thought, human preparation, and human planning will eliminate the presence and power of the Holy Spirit in preaching or worship. Some of us subscribe, perhaps at a very deep and unexpressed level, to the belief that the more we study for a sermon, the less likely it is that God will show up.[5]

Considering human effort to be hostile to the Spirit's work may come from the sincere desire to capture one genuine strand of biblical teaching. As the prophet Zechariah famously declared, "'Not by [human] might nor by [human] power, but by My Spirit,' says the LORD of hosts" (Zech. 4:6 NASB). The Psalmist warns, "Unless the LORD builds the house, They labor in vain" (Ps. 127:1 NASB). The Quietists in Wesley's day often quoted Exodus 14:13–14, "Stand firm, and see the salvation of the LORD, which he will work for you today. . . . Be [still]" (ESV), to prove that God's mighty work emerges only through full human passivity.

Wesley insisted on reading a little further in the story where the Lord commanded Moses and the Israelites, "Go forward. . . . Lift up your staff" (Ex. 14:15–16 ESV). While the command to "be still" proves that only God can save, the command to "go forward" unveils the complementary truth that God acts *through* human action (trust and obedience). In the same vein, the psalmist prayed, "Establish the work of our hands" (Ps. 90:17 AMP), naming human labor as one avenue through which God is pleased to demonstrate His power. These insights have direct bearing on how we prepare to preach. We must put to rest the notion that we prepare better by preparing less or that the truly spiritual preacher is the least studied one. Rather, we can live in the light of Genesis 1, in which God declared all that He had made (including the human being and by implication the human mind) to be "very good" (Gen. 1:31 NIV).[6] We can embrace the full devotion Jesus advocated: "You shall love the Lord your God with all your heart and with all your soul and with all your mind" (Matt. 22:37, quoting Deut. 6:5 AMP). If we surrender to Jesus all that we are, we will be offering to Him the very best our minds can offer, an offering He may be pleased to break, bless, and multiply.[7]

SPIRIT-LED PREACHERS

Nearly all Wesleyans, along with most evangelicals, classify themselves as Arminians, believing human beings are called to embrace the truth of the gospel through the capacity of human "free will." We often name the act of turning to follow Jesus a "choice" or "decision" made by "free moral agents."

Accordingly, we typically envision evangelism as the work of sharing the *information* that God loves us and has provided the means for all of us to reach the blissful realm of heaven. We *explain* the gospel, trying our best to make clear the facts of human need, of divine provision, of the negative consequences of its rejection, and of the overwhelmingly positive benefits of its acceptance. If our listeners hesitate to accept any given point of information, we (ideally) have counterarguments on hand to establish that point through more information or fuller reasoning.

GENTLE

Robert Chiles[8] has argued cogently that trying to convince people into the Kingdom represents an evolution (for the worse) away from the classical Arminianism Wesley embraced. Wesley described himself as largely agreeing with Calvinism's pessimistic view of the human condition apart from God's intervention. The Bible does not describe lost human beings as neutral creatures ready and able to process information fairly or arrive at unbiased conclusions based on a true evaluation of reality. Rather, the sons and daughters of Adam are a dead, blind, and rebellious lot whose view of reality is fundamentally inverted. Human beings in our deadness are numb to truth, in our blindness cannot see it even as we stare at it, and in our rebellion would reject it if we could glimpse its beauty.[9] It is clear that no gospel invitation, however passionately or skillfully presented, will have any chance of breaking through these layers of sinful defense.

Wesley's interpretation of Scripture did not lead him to insist that human *free will* was a fundamental reality of the human condition. Rather he insisted upon the operation of God's *free grace*—a grace set loose by God within the world at large and the human heart in particular—to recreate possibilities for humans to respond rightly to the gospel. Important clues in Scripture point to the Holy Spirit as the agent who is busy undertaking this loving, unilateral action within us: seeking us out, penetrating our defenses, showing us our need, and creating within us the first sparks of interest in and desire for God.[10] Jesus declared the Spirit would "convince the world concerning sin and righteousness and judgment" (John 16:8 RSV), a conviction no doubt designed to open our doors wide enough to admit shafts of true light.[11] Paul reminisced over the conversion of the Thessalonians, recalling that the preaching of the gospel was accompanied with "deep conviction," no doubt a veiled reference to the Spirit of God (1 Thess. 1:5 NIV). As preachers, we are called to depend radically upon the Spirit as the only One able to take our feeble words and impress their truth upon the hearts and minds of our listeners.

UNDER AUTHORITY

Sometimes church architecture communicates amazing truth. In a number of Reformed churches in the Netherlands, one sees the following arrangement at the front of the sanctuary: a table for the Lord's Supper, a basin for the baptismal waters, a lofty pulpit with steep stairs ascending to it, and a long desk with several chairs stationed at the foot of those stairs.

Most of us will make sense of every feature except the table and chairs. A closer look reveals that lying on the table are several sets of books: Bibles and church disciplines, to be exact. Now their function comes into view. At the table sit the elders of the congregation charged with listening to the pastor's sermon to measure it against the Scripture and the teaching of the church. As the pastor descends from the pulpit, the elders meet him either to congratulate him for faithful preaching or to request that he reconsider his claims.[12]

Many of us can imagine the abusive scenes that could take place in these encounters, with mean-spirited church bosses and obstinate laymen venting their opposition to godly pastors. But our fears of power struggles and church meltdowns must not obscure an important biblical teaching represented by this peculiar furniture: the people of God have a responsibility to discern whether God indeed has addressed them through the particular declarations of the one assuming the role of God's prophet.

> But I think the true notion of the Spirit is, that it is some portion of, as well as preparation for, a life in God, which we are to enjoy hereafter. The gift of the Holy Spirit looks full to the resurrection; for then is the life of God completed in us.
>
> —John Wesley, Sermon CXLI, "On the Holy Spirit"

This matter merits careful attention, especially in our climate where pastoral leadership is sometimes defined in authoritarian fashion.[13] As the Israelites transferred their allegiance from Moses (who had just died) to Joshua (their newly designated leader) they declared, "Just as we obeyed Moses in all things, so we will obey you; only may the LORD your God be with you as he was with Moses" (Josh. 1:17 NASB). In other words, their obedience was conditioned upon their discernment that God indeed was *with* Joshua, guiding him as he led the people. Absent their conviction of God's active guidance within Joshua, Israel was not compelled to follow him.

Later, in the new covenant, Paul exhorted the Thessalonian believers to "test everything" (1 Thess. 5: 21). This call stands within Paul's instructions about how God's people should respond to Christian prophets (those who speak God's word to God's people). On the one hand, Paul wanted the Thessalonians to respect and to heed those speaking for God: "Do not quench the Spirit; do not despise prophetic utterances." But immediately he followed this with *complementary* guidance: "Test all things; hold fast what is good, abstain from every form of evil" (RSV). As Gordon Fee demonstrates, the whole people of God must be testing all who claim to speak for God, embracing what passes the test and discarding what doesn't.[14]

Paul urges essentially the same approach with the Corinthians when instructing them how to regulate Christian prophecy. The twin concerns of orderliness and validity emerge from his words, "Let two or three prophets speak, and let the others *weigh* what is said" (1 Cor. 14:29 RSV, italics added). We must note that the work of "weighing" necessarily involves sifting and evaluating, not so as to question God, but to gain the assurance that God indeed has so spoken. In other words, "weighing" protects the interests of God, holds prophets accountable to God, and requires the participation of God's people in discerning the true will and purposes of God.[15]

These texts together demonstrate that preaching which dares to speak for God and reveal the will of God takes place safely only when accompanied by genuine community evaluation of it. Pastors who refuse to submit their visions and plans to the congregation are (in effect) denying the presence of the Spirit within the people of God and the necessary gift of discernment alive among them. Congregations who refuse to take up the responsibility of evaluating their leaders and preachers according to the Word of God are exposing themselves to the dangers of discernment by a single individual. Blessed are those moments when preacher and people together recognize what the Spirit is saying to the church.

EMPOWERED

Contemporary culture often celebrates the resilient human spirit and tells stirring stories of determination in the face of impossible odds. Our heroes are the athletes, soldiers, and civil servants who overcome huge resistance to win the prize, seize the hill, or rescue the victim. We are especially touched when someone who has been stricken with a devastating handicap keeps grinding forward to achieve the unimaginable.

We can learn valuable lessons from such courageous examples, and recognize many glimmerings of God's grace at work throughout our world. Whenever people choose to sacrifice for others, to work for the common good, to embrace optimism rather than bitterness, we can be sure that the Father of Light is at work, not the Prince of Darkness.[16]

At the same time, our culture expresses far too grand a confidence in human will, in human vision, and in human ability. Throughout the pages of Scripture we humans are portrayed as *weak* and *limited*. Unflatteringly, we are compared to "dust," to "mist," and to "grass"—certainly not to shame us but to expose the foolishness of any imagined self-sufficiency.

Repeatedly in 1 and 2 Corinthians, Paul set forth a vision of Christian ministry that was unattractive to most in his culture and no doubt repulsive to many in ours. In contrast to some who preached the gospel, he came to town "in weakness" (1 Cor. 2:3), believing God's power came into view only when he embraced his own weakness. "For when I am weak, then I am strong" (2 Cor. 12:10). Turning his attention to the Corinthians themselves, he noted their lowly social status, "Not many of you were wise according to worldly standards, not many were powerful, not many were of noble birth; but God chose what is foolish in the world to shame the wise, God chose what is weak in the world to shame the strong . . . so that no human being might boast in the presence of God. . . . Let him who boasts, boast in the Lord" (from 1 Cor. 1:26–31 RSV).

> By renewing men and women, by bringing about their new solidarity and fellowship, and by delivering the body from death, the Holy Spirit glorifies the risen Lord and, through him, the Father. This glorification of the Father through the Son in the Spirit is the consummation of creation. It expresses its perfect joy in eternal rejoicing.
>
> —Jürgen Moltmann,
> *The Trinity and the Kingdom*

Paul was not advocating that we collapse on the floor in a puddle of failure. He expected powerful results from his ministry but not by reaching deep within inside himself to tap into "the human spirit" or "rock-solid determination." To the Philippians he declared, "I can do all things . . . in him who strengthens me" (Phil. 4:13 RSV). To the Colossians he remarked, "For [the previously stated goal] I toil, striving with all the energy which he mightily inspires within me" (Col. 1:29 RSV). The apostle did not envision himself as a passive pawn used by an overpowering God apart from his own will and work. But he did consider his own will and effort to be sponsored by, and then swept up into, the larger purposes of God. Paul was not a self-made wonder but God's "workmanship" (Eph. 2:10 RSV). These matters converge in the event of preaching. If our preaching calls for decision, for change, for action, for transformation and renewal, then we are stepping into that puzzling mystery of how the human will is moved, and then how good intentions can be converted into actual behavior. We preachers are indeed exhorting the human will, but even more crucially we are calling upon the Spirit of God, God's empowering presence[17], to reveal and convince, to strengthen and enable.[18] Our prayers, our very mindset, and our explicit language in preaching must invoke the Holy Spirit whose presence and power alone can enliven the body of Christ for life and ministry fully pleasing to the Father.

Ours is a day when the doctrine of the Trinity is being revitalized across the Christian spectrum, when both the academic and ecclesial worlds are rediscovering the bond between Trinitarian worship and vital Christian living. We who labor in The Wesleyan Church need to refocus a keen sense of the Holy Spirit's presence and purposes. By recovering a Trinitarian vision of Christian faith and practice, we can approach again that holy ground where we can hear and proclaim what the Spirit is saying to the churches (Rev. 2:7, 11, 17, 29; 3:6, 13, 22).

ACTION SUGGESTIONS

Ask yourself the following questions. Don't allow yourself to leave them until you have reached real and reasonably complete answers:

1. Why and how do I choose the texts for my preaching? Am I using them to deliver points I already know I want to make, or am I surrendering in fresh ways to the light of the Word upon my own life and upon the lives of my people?

2. Upon whom am I really relying to bring about an effective response among my listeners? How might I tease out differences between what I say my answer is and what my practices, moods, and strategies might suggest as the real answer(s)?

3. Do I have a radical trust in the Word of God to be relevant to our lives today, or have I cast myself into the role of somehow making the Bible relevant? Could a deeper trust in and engagement with Scripture allow me to preach and teach with more confidence so that, through the Spirit, it speaks to the deep issues of human hearts and lives?

FOR FURTHER READING

Jones, J. Ithel. *The Holy Spirit and Christian Preaching*. London: Epworth Press, 1967.

Jones deals here with the mystery of the faith and the mystery of preaching, mysteries compounded by the nature of the Holy Spirit's ministry, which always points toward the "Eternal Son."

Kinlaw, Dennis F. *Preaching in the Spirit*. Wilmore: Francis Asbury Press, 1985.

Dennis Kinlaw is one of the giants of the Wesleyan/Holiness movement of the last half-century. In this book he deals with the purpose of preaching and other issues of importance both to the preacher and to the hearer.

Oden, Thomas C. *Life in the Spirit*. New York: HarperCollins Publishers, 1992.

This is volume three of Oden's systematic theology, and an excellent treatment of Christian/historical/Wesleyan teaching on the Holy Spirit.

NOTES

1. Dennis F. Kinlaw, *Preaching in the Spirit* (Wilmore: Francis Asbury Press, 1985), 10.

2. This story was related to me by the Rev. Dr. David Handy in informal conversation on the campus of Union Theological Seminary in Richmond, VA, in the fall of 1986.

3. The Holy Spirit is described in Acts about fifteen times as playing some role within the life of the nascent church.

4. A line often repeated in his preaching by Dr. J. R. Mitchell. My primary exposure to him was from May, 1993, to May, 1994, at Stonewall Wesleyan Church, Lexington, KY.

5. We all have stories of how the Holy Spirit moved in an unusual way right in the midst of poor performance or lack of preparation. But these exceptional moments cannot establish for us a new "method" for guaranteeing the Spirit's action.

6. It certainly is true that the fall of humankind in the garden plunged us into darkness and brought about a distortion of our capacities, including those of the mind. It is also true that the gracious work of God has set about restoring what sin has distorted. One dimension of the Christian's renewal is the renewal of the "mind" (Rom. 12:1–2), enabling us (if not requiring us) to harness our best thinking for the service of Christ.

7. John R. W. Stott, *Your Mind Matters: The Place of the Mind in the Christian Life* (Downers Grove: InterVarsity Press, 1972), 96.

8. Robert E. Chiles, "Methodist Apostasy from Free Grace to Free Will," *Religion in Life* XXVII, no. 3 (1958): passim.

9. John 8:31–34; 9:39–41; Rom. 1:18–21; 5:10; 6:20; 1 Cor. 2:14–16; Eph. 2:1–10, and other like passages, describe the sinful human condition in terms far more serious than guilt (i.e. liability to future punishment). We are described as blind, insensitive, enslaved, hostile, undiscerning, and unresponsive. The fundamental distortion of our ability to recognize truth makes the (unaided) gospel preacher unable to engage us effectively.

10. The Spirit does not force a positive response to the gospel, though an initial and unilateral work of the Spirit is necessary before we can muster any positive response. Apparently, the Spirit's work can be "successfully" (sadly!) resisted (see, e.g., Acts 7:51).

11. It is interesting that D. A. Carson, who tends to adopt traditional Calvinist interpretations, concludes (as do we) that this passage in John's Gospel describes the Spirit's convicting role as a positive one, designed to lead sinners to repentance; D. A. Carson, *The Gospel According to John* (Grand Rapids: Wm. B. Eerdmans, 1991), 532–542.

12. Donald J. Bruggink and Carl H. Droppers, *Christ and Architecture: Building Presbyterian/Reformed Churches*, (Grand Rapids: Eerdmans, 1965), 338–351. The

authors declare, "By the work of the Holy Spirit, and the appointment of men (usually as in Acts 14:23, by the vote of the congregation), elders are taken from the midst of the congregation and given these high duties. . . . The Church is not at the whim of the minister; he is not allowed to teach and preach as he alone wishes. No, the elders, reading their Bibles and studying their Doctrinal Standards, are given the responsibility for the right proclamation of the Word" (339–40).

13. Our interest here is not to engage the larger issue of leadership style, biblical or otherwise. Our interest lies solely in asking whether congregations have a responsibility to evaluate pastoral faithfulness to the Word of God. In a parallel fashion, the process toward ordination involves the judgment of congregational and district representatives regarding the fitness and giftedness of individuals for ministry. No minister is to be ordained simply upon his or her demand to be ordained, based on a sense of calling guaranteed solely by the candidate. This communal discernment does not stem from contemporary cultural or democratic ideals but from biblical clues suggesting that the people of God must play a role in the identification, ordination, and evaluation of its ministers.

14. See Gordon D. Fee, *God's Empowering Presence: The Holy Spirit in the Letters of Paul* (Peabody: Hendrickson Publishers, 1994), 55–62, for an excellent treatment of the details of this passage.

15. It is even appropriate to translate "weighing" as "judging." See B. Gartner, "Distinguish, Doubt," in *The New International Dictionary of New Testament Theology, Vol. 1* (Grand Rapids: Zondervan, 1975), 503.

16. One of the beauties of the doctrine of prevenient grace is the permission it gives us to thank God for, and rejoice in, all good dimensions of life and society . . . even those not directly generated by Christian people. We need not paint everything outside the church with a tar brush, since we know that "every good and perfect gift is from above" (James 1:17).

17. We take this phrase from the title of Fee's book.

18. It may be helpful to define "moralistic" preaching. In our estimation, such preaching constantly calls people to "be good," to "do better," and "help others." The problem with such preaching is not that its general goals are evil, but that it fails to ground all moral exhortation in what God already has done through Christ, in who believers are in Christ, and in how the enabling presence of the Holy Spirit makes holy living possible.

STRANGE BUT TRUE

An Epistemological Reminder

Carlton Fisher

*How, then, can they call on the one they have not believed in? And how can
they believe in the one of whom they have not heard? And how can they hear
without someone preaching to them?. . . Consequently, faith comes from
hearing the message, and the message is heard through the word of Christ.*

—Romans 10:14, 17

*Praise the Father of Lights, who hath opened the eyes of our understanding,
to discern those things which could not be seen by eyes of flesh and blood;
that He who of old time shined out of darkness, hath shined in our
hearts, and enlightened us with the light of the glory of God,
in the face of Jesus Christ, "the author and finisher of our faith."*

—John Wesley, Sermon XXII, "On Faith"

I n my brief pastoral experience, I found reliable joy in the serving
of the bread and wine of the Lord's Supper. I don't think I enjoyed
any pastoral task so much as this—offering the nourishment of the
broken body and shed blood of Christ to my brothers and sisters who
came to eat and drink complete with their struggles and doubts. Real
food and real drink for real life.

Or so I believed.

I believe some *very* strange things. If you are a Christian pastor, so do you. I think about these strange things when I am watching people in church waiting in line to tear off a small piece of bread, dip it into a cup, and solemnly eat it while returning to their seats.

I first experienced this method of receiving the communion meal (called "intinction") when I began attending Houghton Wesleyan Church. While unusual to me at first, this way to experience the Lord's Supper has become my favorite. The change occurred during a difficult period when I was not very happy with some of the people waiting in line with me; I realized that no matter what separated me from them, something far more important—and wonderfully strange—bound us together. We shared a worldview that made sense out of standing in line, tearing off a small piece of bread, dipping it into a cup, and eating it.

It's not just that we *did* it; it is what we *believed* we were doing when doing it. Those people in that line—some good friends, some sources of irritation or pain, some complete strangers—*believed* that the death and resurrection of Jesus of Nazareth is *the* single most important event in the history of the world. We believed that in following His command to remember that event by eating and drinking in this way we accept another portion of divine grace into our lives, lives made more abundant thereby.

And as I watched, I thought: All these people *believe* this stuff? This is strange. They are strange. Yes, I, too, am strange for believing as they do. I am one of them; we are strange. Brothers and sisters we are, members of a strange and peculiar group.

And sometimes, since I am cursed with a philosophical bent, I ask myself *why* we believe this strangeness.

THAT WHICH WE KNOW

The gospel is strange: a stumbling block to the Jews, foolishness to the Greeks. Yet familiarity with it over the years can breed a sense of obviousness. The repetition of the words, the well-worn sound of central biblical texts, the settled conviction in our hearts and minds of their truthfulness, can conspire to make the truly remarkable seem self-evident. And this can breed a sort of contempt for those who do not believe it.

But it must not be. Never must the preacher allow conviction of the truth of the message to hide the basic fact that the message proclaimed is beyond the capacity of human cognition. Unaided, we simply *cannot* know it is true.

I need to be careful here. I happen to have a very high view of human cognitive abilities. Many things intimately related to the gospel we can know. By "know" I do not mean "drop-dead certain, with no room for doubt or possibility of error." I mean, instead, what we typically mean when we affirm that human beings know a great deal, most of which is less than certain. We can know that God exists and a fair amount about what God is like. We can know that causing harm to our neighbors is morally wrong. We can know that Jesus of Nazareth was one of the most remarkable and influential men ever to have lived. We have natural abilities to understand, to believe, to know all these things. (Of course, these natural abilities—like our natural abilities to digest, procreate, and see—have supernatural origins.)

The gospel, however, is different: "The Word became flesh and lived for awhile among us." "God was in Christ, reconciling the world to himself." "To all who received [Jesus], to those who believed in his name, he gave the right to become children of God." "There is now no condemnation for those who are in Christ Jesus." "But, if you confess with your mouth, 'Jesus is Lord,' and believe in your heart that God raised him from the dead, you will be saved." These claims, and much else found in Scripture, simply cannot be known by human beings under normal circumstances. Furthermore, unlike much human knowledge, comprehension of these claims is nontransferable. Hearing them from someone "in the know" is never enough.

Think of how we typically come to know things. Much is via our senses; we *see* our best friend who has just driven into our driveway. Some of it is via a direct operation of reason. We are able to *see*—with our minds, not our eyes—that if Sue is taller than Bob, and Jake is taller than Sue, then Jake must be taller than Bob. With our senses we have access to the physical world. With our reason we have access to a world of conceptual relationships—we do math; we make inferences. A third type of knowledge involves our internal lives—what we think, how we feel. We may use "introspection" as a name for the faculty via which we know such things.

A vast amount of what we know, however, does not come from any of these three sources, at least not directly. Much of what we know, perhaps most, comes through what others tell us. We watch the news; we read papers, magazines, and books; we gain news by word-of-mouth. Of course, hearing and reading utilizes our senses, and the messengers may have learned what they tell us via sense, reason, or introspection. But that is beside the point; *we* rely on *their* testimony.

This reliance on the testimony of others for information is central in human relationships and in how we construct our lives. It is why truth-telling is a moral imperative. And preaching would appear to be a form of testimony, one human talking to others with the goal of stimulating belief, igniting passion, and motivating action. But when preachers aim for passion and action without a prior effort to share knowledge with their listeners, they show disrespect. Christian passion and action must be grounded in truth; manipulation and propaganda must be avoided.

THREE LEVELS OF UNDERSTANDING

A preacher can communicate truth to the congregation on various levels. The first level of understanding is based simply on the testimony of the preacher. When the preacher tells a personal story, the listener is asked to accept the report. If the preacher illustrates a point by describing a current or historical event, the hearer should be able to rely on the accuracy of the description. When the preacher shares the results of a scholarly inquiry into the historical or linguistic context of the text, the listener is asked to believe what the preacher says. Common to all "testimonial transfers" of knowledge from one person to another is the requirement of trust. The hearer must trust that the speaker knows the information and is reporting it honestly.

The second level is not the take-my-word-on-this sort. Instead it is: "Look. Do you *see* this? Do you understand now?" The goal of the exposition of a passage of Scripture is to elicit an *ah-ha* moment: "Yes! *That* is what it is teaching here." Somewhat analogous to this would be the learning of elementary arithmetic, when the student passes from *accepting* the teacher's word that 7+5=12 to actually *understanding* that it is so. In this second kind of learning, the preacher no longer poses as the authority but creates an occasion for the hearer to see the truth directly—a truth that can be remembered, even passed along without the preface, "My preacher said . . ."

Insofar as a primary task of the preacher is to exposit the Scripture so the congregation can understand it and be better prepared to read it for themselves with understanding, this is a skill the good preacher will have developed quite fully. Yet notice that the content of such understanding is generally about what the Bible teaches. It is not yet the belief that what the Bible teaches is *true*. Most specifically, it is not belief in the *gospel*, the belief that brings new life.

So we come back to the heart of the matter, the strange beliefs that set apart the peculiar people of God. These beliefs are not accessible via our senses, our reason, or our introspection. Neither can they be transferred from preacher to listener via testimony—no sensible person *should* believe these seemingly crazy things just because someone says they are true. These beliefs require something more—a third level of understanding that is the goal of the preacher but outside the preacher's control.

Preaching, for its most significant success, cannot rely on either the preacher's trustworthiness in testifying or persuasiveness in explaining. Preachers should know what they are talking about, should have studied the passage thoroughly, should be able to give personal witness to the truths as they intersect with current human life, and should carefully invite the listener to understand what the text is saying. Preachers should have the intellectual, moral, and spiritual character to qualify as someone worthy of hearing. But the messages preachers ultimately wish to communicate are ones that even they cannot know without a work of God; and it requires a similar work in the mind of the hearer for the hearer to gain understanding. Authentic faith cannot come second-hand.

EPIPHANY

Christians speak sometimes about "making the faith one's own," referring to thoughtful reflection on what one has been taught, deciding whether to continue believing it or not. I whole-heartedly embrace the sentiment here, but it inevitably comes up short against the obvious truth that an adult—whether young, mature, or retired—is no more capable than a child of judging whether Jesus is God's incarnate Word.

Consider the account of Thomas found in John's gospel. It may be fair to say Thomas doubted; it is not fair to say Jesus criticized him for it. Thomas was absent when the resurrected Jesus appeared to the other disciples. We don't know why he was not there; hence, we don't know whether his absence was a source of culpability. We do know his absence created a problem. Yes, the other disciples testified to Thomas; but can you really find reason to condemn Thomas for not taking their word?

Jesus, previewing the way He would show grace to succeeding generations, appeared again when Thomas was present. He provided Thomas with the same evidence He had given the others. He offered His hands and side for Thomas' probing inspection. It was certainly all right with Jesus for Thomas to use all his powers to understand and to know in his attempt to respond. According to the text, Thomas did not need to touch; seeing was sufficient for satisfying his inquiring mind.

But notice Thomas' exclamation: "My Lord and my God!" On what basis did he make *that* claim? Was he able to see it was true—with his eyes? No. At best, he could see Jesus was alive. Was he able to reason that since Jesus was alive, He must be God? Thomas had witnessed enough to know Jesus was amazingly and wonderfully different. And now this! Thomas should have been open to a discussion of the matter. But reason did not compel this conclusion. As amazing as any resurrection would be, it is not proof that the one raised is the Eternal Word. Nor could Thomas make this affirmation of faith on the basis of his internal emotional reaction to seeing the risen Christ, no matter the level of ecstasy he may have felt.

So what did enable Thomas to utter this confession, the affirmation that opened for him the door to life eternal? Or better, Who enabled him? "For it is by grace [we] have been saved, through faith—and this not from [our]selves, it is the gift of God." Thomas made a leap to a conclusion he could not have reached on his own. He had a moment of extreme clarity regarding Jesus: an epiphany. He was able to "see" the truth because God gifted him with this ability. Whether it is this initial insight of faith or one of countless other affirmations and reaffirmations the Spirit of God may help us make, facilitating moments like this is the goal of preaching.

THE ROLE OF THE PREACHER

As the Spirit is the only One able to create this kind of understanding in a person, what is the role of the preacher in facilitating epiphanies?

First, the preacher brings the message of Another. Since God convicts us of the truth of God's Word, it must be God's Word the preacher proclaims. It is God's Word that will not be fruitless, even though much of the soil it falls on is hard and stony. The pulpit is not a forum for expressing personal opinion or a platform for entertaining—though strong views and funny stories may be shared from the pulpit if the specific purpose is to open up the truth of the Word.

The preacher is an emissary, an ambassador. The *sermon* may be created by the preacher, but the *message* must not be. The message is from the King. Just as political ambassadors must show their credentials, so must Christian preachers—by keeping the biblical text at the very center of the sermon and making utterly clear to the listener that they submit to the authority of the text.

Second, the preacher embraces the strangeness. No matter how many years ago the preacher's own epiphany occurred, the strangeness of the message must not be forgotten. Daily, the preacher must meet the Lord so as to marvel continuously at the message. The preacher cannot forget how the good news must sound to nonbelievers; this story about the Word becoming flesh, God humbling himself to become a man, and dying an ignoble death so humans might live sounds like foolishness. The preacher cannot forget how even believers who have enjoyed moments of great clarity also experience seasons of doubt when they simultaneously testify and plead, "Lord, I believe; help thou my unbelief."

Third, the preacher must teach—making every effort to make sense of the message. The preacher never revels in the strangeness of the gospel as though *that's* why we believe it. The difficulty in believing it is not the indicator of its truth. There is no excuse for avoiding the hard work of providing those who listen a breathtaking sight into the most coherent, honest, ennobling, and hope-filled view of reality the world ever has known. Paul says people cannot be expected to believe without a preacher. At times I wonder whether faith can come *with* a preacher. Why isn't teaching a preferred method of communicating the Word to people? Instead of an approach that says, "You all be quiet and listen to me until I'm done—and then leave," wouldn't it be more helpful, more respectful, to explain something and then entertain questions, musing together about difficult issues?

This was the question of a college student—me—who had never preached. When, a few years later, I began preaching, I understood the answer. Now I listen to sermons knowing something of the burden, and privilege, of preparing and preaching them. I still value teaching (it's no accident I became a teacher) but the oral communication I most admire is a deeply prepared, clearly conceived, artfully constructed, and powerfully delivered sermon in which the very voice of God can be heard. I think I have done it—or, more modestly, *almost* done it—a very few times. I know something of how hard it is. I've tasted the joy that can accompany it. I have felt what a heavy responsibility it brings (and what it feels like not to have shouldered that responsibility well). Therein lies the difference between teaching and preaching. The teacher says, "Come, let us reason together"; the preacher says, "Listen, I have a word from God."

Thus, even when we avoid the error of thinking that sermons cause epiphanies, it turns out the preacher's words are very important. The role of the preacher is divinely assigned. How else will they hear?

COOPERATING WITH THE SPIRIT

I was fortunate to attend church in London for nearly a year, a Church of England parish with a vigorous evangelical message, All Souls, Langham Place, where John Stott pastored for years. I enjoyed the most consistently good preaching I have ever heard from about a half dozen members of the staff. (Yes, fewer sermons to prepare can have a positive effect on the quality of each.) A common request in prayer during the service was that God would help the preacher as he explained the scripture passage to us. What a simple and elegant way to refer to the masterful presentation we soon would hear: an explanation of the scripture.

Have I now contradicted myself? How can I suggest it is the preacher's task to explain the word, the gospel, the message—to "make sense of it" for the listener—after having said the message is so strange its content is beyond the range of human faculties? If it cannot be understood and embraced unless the Spirit enables, how can it be the preacher's task to explain it?

Remember, the preacher is supposed to be in a "privileged epistemological position." (This is the position you are in, for example, when you have a toothache. No matter the opinion of anyone else to the contrary, *you* know you are in pain!) Just because the truths of the gospel cannot be known and understood without the direct activity of the Spirit of God doesn't mean the preacher doesn't know them. Nor does it mean the preacher cannot have a deep understanding of them. Quite the opposite is supposed to be the case. For centuries, thoughtful Christians have been seeking understanding of what they have come to know by faith—and with remarkable success.

We believe the Spirit helps us understand texts as we study them and pray over them. The preacher's words are never sufficient for the task at hand; God still must work in the ears and minds of the hearers. But this does not free the preacher to be careless or lazy. The requirement of the preacher is still to explain, delivering the message accurately and clearly. Preachers have a coherent and fresh message because they have spent time prayerfully and thoughtfully in the text.

All preachers know the difference between going into the pulpit believing they have a word from God and going in with . . . well, with something far less. (Remember, a "word from God" is insight into the meaning of the text, not a new text.)

Consider again Thomas' encounter with the risen Lord. Though showing the wounds to Thomas was not in itself sufficient to convince him, still, Jesus' disclosure *was* an important part of the process. Can you imagine Jesus laughing off Thomas's inquiring mind, his serious and legitimate questions: "Oh, Thomas, why are you so hung up on evidence? Why do you insist on thinking so much? Don't you know you can never figure this out on your own? You need a divine gift truly to believe. Forget the questions; here, take the gift."

We cannot really imagine that scenario because Jesus does not treat our capacities for inquiry—the ones He designed and gave us—with such disdain. They may not be sufficient, but they are to be fully deployed. "Here, Thomas, put your hand into my side."

The preacher should treat the congregation as Jesus treated Thomas. No one can affirm the truth clearly without God's help. No one can understand *fully,* even with God's help. Even the preacher looks through a darkened glass. But the preacher *does* see; the preacher *does* know; the preacher *can* make *some* sense of it all—or else the preacher is not yet ready for the pulpit.

So the preacher, as it were, shows the nail prints in Jesus' hands and the gash of the spear in His side. With clarity the preacher explains the text. With imagination the preacher anticipates the questions of bright Thomas and others like him sitting in the pews. With passion, preachers claim to know what they are talking about, that the message really is from God. With perceptivity the preacher suggests how the text is applied with relevance in the current age. With every intellectual resource that can be summoned, the preacher brings the hearer as close as humanly possible to the very brink—and then, trusting, leaves the person in God's hands.

Since it is God's part to grant the gift of faith, the preacher can preach with confidence. Even though the preacher doesn't have to close the deal, so to speak, the preacher's task is not easy. No doubt every preacher has wished on some days that God would choose an easier venue as the means to His grace. Other venues exist—Bible reading, baptism, the Eucharist. Why are those not sufficient?

But how will they hear, without a preacher, without someone delivering the word?

And how will they believe—really *believe*—even *with* a preacher?

By a miracle of God's grace.

It is the combination of Word and Spirit. If it were not for the revelation in Scripture, we would not even be aware of the gospel; and if it were not for the activity of the Holy Spirit in our hearts and minds, we would not be persuaded of its truth.

The preacher declares, "Thus saith the Lord"; the Spirit whispers, "'Tis true."

ACTION SUGGESTIONS

Questions to ask when preparing to enter the pulpit:

1. Do I have a word from God? Can I locate this word in the Word? Am I truly just the messenger of Another?

2. Do I appreciate the degree to which this word is foolishness—countercultural, beyond our ability to figure out on our own?

3. Still, by God's grace, do I grasp it? Even if I can't understand it fully, can I place it within a coherent, compelling, and hope-filled vision of the world and what God is doing in it? Am I ready to explain it? Can I resist the impulse merely to glory in the mystery and, instead, respect the intellect of my listeners as they ask sensible questions?

4. Do I have the intellectual, moral, and spiritual character to qualify as someone worthy of being heard?

5. Am I ready to trust God to work in the lives of my listeners? Do I realize that any belief that results from my own articulate persuasiveness alone will not yet be full faith?

FOR FURTHER READING

Two volumes of recent, serious philosophical work in the epistemology of Christian belief, and God's voice in Scripture:

Plantinga, Alvin. *Warranted Christian Belief.* Oxford: Oxford University Press, 2000.

For those willing to wade into deep philosophical waters, this work in the epistemology of Christian belief by America's foremost Christian philosopher explores how our Christian beliefs are "warranted." Included in this study are the role of Scripture and the witness of the Holy Spirit.

Wolterstorff, Nicholas. *Divine Discourse.* Cambridge: Cambridge University Press, 1995.

Could it be that God actually *speaks* to us through these ancient texts? And can we believe this in our postmodern age in which the meaning of authors is believed to be so fully obscured by the interpretation of the reader (of any text)? Find in this text a philosophical argument for understanding scripture as God's word to us.

Two important works on Christian preaching:

Craddock, Fred B. *Preaching.* Nashville: Abingdon Press, 1985.

Read this book by one of today's leading preachers and theoreticians to get behind the "How to?" of preaching to the "Why?" What is the theology of God's choice of preaching as the major vehicle for delivery of the gospel message?

Long, Thomas G. *Testimony: Talking Ourselves into Being Christian.* San Francisco: Jossey-Bass, 2004.

This book explores how we communicate the *information* of the faith to one another. What peculiar role does our use of words in testimony play in the Christian life?

A SERMON TAKES A WEEK

Preparation

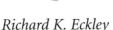

Richard K. Eckley

Cheap grace is the preaching of forgiveness without requiring repentance, baptism without church discipline, Communion without confession, absolution without personal confession. Cheap grace is grace without discipleship, grace without the cross, grace without Jesus Christ, living and incarnate.

—Dietrich Bonhoeffer, *The Cost of Discipleship*

I was more convinced than ever that the preaching like an Apostle, without joining together those that are awakened and training them up in the ways of God, is only begetting children for the murderer.

—John Wesley, Journal entry, August 25, 1763

Late on a Saturday night a minister, under great stress and apprehension, is found preparing the Lord's Day sermon in the fluorescent glow of his office. As he types, the words on the monitor look something like what he had thought he would say, but he knows he will have to rest upon his sheer skills as a communicator, yet again, to pull this off. The Bible lies open on his desk, evading a serious probing; most of the ideas now flowing from his fingers are rehashed stories he's picked up from the Internet and a monthly sermon flyer. Sticky-notes lining the sides of his desk remind him that plenty of other items have forced themselves into that hour of worship: an extended medley by the worship team; announcements of worship team practices, age-level choir auditions, and a myriad of other meetings—missions committees, master planning for the church, and staff development. Last on his to-do list of preparations is before him now, and he doesn't like what he sees.

A few years earlier this same minister had been at a pastor's conference and found himself in a transparent moment with his roommate. He'd told this colleague from a neighboring church, point-blank, "My preaching has really taken a nose dive. We've turned the focus of our morning service to worship, so my sermon has not really been that important anymore." The two of them had commiserated and promised to hold each other accountable for prioritizing their sermon preparation in their weekly duties.

Now he laughs to himself. "What was I thinking? This is the real world. No one has the luxury of spending that much time on a piece of oration no one listens to anyway." The pastor turns off the lights in his office and walks through the stage area of his sanctuary. The pulpit looks small and puny, lost in the midst of instruments, screens, and lights. The table for the Lord's Supper is covered in microphone cords, and the printed sermon in his hand doesn't seem to measure up to the high-tech delivery before him.

"Maybe next week," he tells himself.

THE SHIFTING PRIORITY OF THE SERMON

No one would doubt the temptations upon contemporary preachers to relegate sermons to the back burner in the allocation of their energies. Most would agree that the new emphasis upon vital and vibrant music has enhanced the church venue for a scrutinizing public. At the same time, this modernization has dislodged the Word from being the centerpiece it once was. Discovering the role preaching should properly play in today's worship might bring a renewed sense that the sermon does not stand alone, that it is an essential part of the total worship experience, and that it is at the core of the Church's self-understanding.

The place of the sermon in Sunday morning worship certainly has changed since the Reformation. The Greek text of Erasmus became the source of power for the Reforming preachers. Luther's German translation kick-started an unstoppable force of church reform. Calvin was known for his book-by-book study of the Word, often spending months in the same chapter of the Bible.[1] Through the following centuries, this Protestant emphasis supported many great pulpiteers, perpetuating revivals and waves of spiritual growth.

Even until a short generation ago, one hour of sermon study for every minute in the pulpit was a rule of thumb in many seminary homiletics classes. Elements of the service other than the sermon were added impromptu, unrehearsed. Few pastors or worship leaders (song leaders, they were called then) gave much thought to transitional liturgical features. The sermon was expected to prop up any weaknesses these "interruptions" had brought to the service. People came to hear the Word; all else was merely peripheral.

The great evangelists generally used music as a way of setting the stage for the receptivity of the audience. The ratio of time given to music and to sermon in those ministries, from the days of Whitefield and Wesley through about the midpoint of Graham's career, highlights the superior place of the sermon.

The present-day church often experiences just the opposite in worship. The balance between Word and Sacrament, or between the explanation and the experience of God's mystery, now teeters away from the pulpit. The new celebratory music has displaced the old meditative organ preludes. After lengthy periods of singing to a rhythmic cadence—generally given the production terminology of "sets" and "segues"—the minister is ushered on to provide a talking point before the worship team is let loose upon the congregation for yet another round of singing. The sermon is as much an interlude today as music was a preliminary in days gone by.

The purpose of this chapter is to set forth and explain the liturgical place of the sermon. The concentric nature of the biblical word event will be developed to show that the sermon is larger than the half-hour or so in which it is delivered. This arrangement may be expressed as a series of concentric circles.

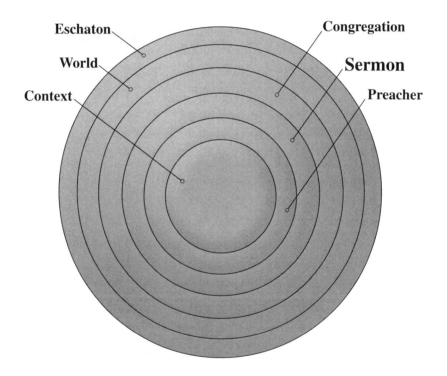

The sermon is forged in the spiritual life of the pastor's week. This is represented by the first, second, and third rings of our circle. As the pastor lives in the community, responds to the pastoral needs of the flock, and discovers God in his or her own spiritual devotion and study, the sermon is percolated and fostered.

The fourth ring of the circle represents the curricular and spiritual formation mechanisms at work as the preacher seeks to connect the congregation with the Church apostolic (what was once called the catechism.) This includes the need to look at the total liturgy, including the order of worship and the worship context.

The fifth and sixth rings represent the *telos* of the sermon as an eschatological event—a connection with the church universal and a celebration of Christ's agenda to heal the world and all its broken systems. The sermon is a bridge to the already-but-not-yet of the Kingdom.

Though this continuum really is an unbroken extension of pastoral theology,[2] to emphasize the role preaching plays in the process we will look at the place of the sermon, its function in congregational worship, and the ultimate purpose of preaching—the transformation of God's people and the world.

PLACE—THE CONTEXT OF THE SERMON

When we talk about the "place" of the sermon we really are pointing to what the Church historically has called its "liturgy." Liturgy (*leitourgia*) is a Greek composite word originally meaning a "public duty," a service to the state undertaken by a citizen. Paul urged Christians to "offer your bodies as living sacrifices, holy and pleasing to God—this is your spiritual act of worship (*leitourgia*)" (Rom. 12:1). We call our worship a "service" because it is an act before God in the public life. Paul, however, understood that service to extend also to the very offering of our lives before God, in a truly public way, in every part and aspect of the Christian's life.

The public setting for the sermon is one of the distinctive and historic contours of Wesleyan preaching. Beginning in Bristol, John Wesley increasingly addressed the public in open areas, giving rise to what early Methodists called "field preaching." On visits back to Epworth he would deliver sermons from the Market Cross in the center of the town. For the rest of his life, Wesley would preach to these public square crowds, often numbering many thousands, throughout Britain and Ireland. Early on he noted:

> I could scarcely reconcile myself at first to this strange way of preaching in the fields, of which Whitfield set me an example on Sunday; having been all my life (till very lately) so tenacious of every point relating to decency and order, that I should have thought the saving of souls almost a sin, if it had not been done in a church.[3]

Wesley is said to have preached forty thousand sermons and to have traveled 250,000 miles. In response to the constraints the ecclesial structures would have placed on his preaching, Wesley explained, "I look upon the whole world as my parish."[4] One would hope that today, as well, the intersection of the church culture with the public culture would be a prominent feature of Wesleyan preaching.

> "Know the Word,
> Teach the Word,
> Preach the Word,
> Defend the Word,
> Incarnate the Word,
> Live the Word."
>
> —William Stringfellow

Because the sermon is forged in the place where people live, the preacher must be shaped by the serious study of the culture of our times as well as of the first-century milieu of the gospel. The British evangelical preacher John R. W. Stott has written, "We cannot afford to remain on either side of the cultural divide. To withdraw from the world into the Bible (which is escapism), or from the Bible into the world (which is conformity), will be fatal to our preaching ministry."[5]

Wesley, a self-proclaimed "Man of One Book," filled his mind with the stream of intellectual literature flowing from the Oxford curriculum, and he included in his library the deep spiritual traditions of the church's saints and mystics. On one occasion Wesley chided a Methodist preacher for his inattention to reading: "I scarce ever knew a preacher read so little. And perhaps by neglecting it you have lost the taste for it. Hence your talent in preaching does not increase. [Your preaching] is just the same as it was seven years ago. It is lively, but not deep."[6]

Reading will deepen the well from which the preacher can drink. It will be perceived by listeners as a natural artesian spring. Pumping the well dry, conversely, churns up the same tired clichés.

The world is one inescapable context for good biblical preaching. But more immediately, this context is not merely the world at large. In a sense, the sermon really comes from the life of the people the pastor most represents. In the sermon, the preacher must flesh out that life with friends, family, and the fellowship of the community. Dietrich Bonhoeffer said it this way: "The pastor, and particularly the young pastor, suffers from being by himself. . . . Preaching which has its roots in practical work, as well as in the life and experience of community, will be more relevant and less likely to run the risk of either being intimidated or bogged down."[7]

PARTICIPATION—THE WORD IN WORSHIP

Following the preacher's immersion into both the culture and the text comes the need to position the preaching event in the life of the congregation, for it is from Scripture that the church comes to drink. As Skudlarek has observed, "The preacher's primary obligation is not to solve people's problems or answer their questions, but to hear the scriptures as God's living word."[8]

Real vibrancy cannot be found in a congregation unless the text is embodied throughout the church. Wesley understood the danger of immediate responses to sermons and worship without the follow-up of discipling ministries: "I was more convinced than ever that the preaching like an Apostle, without joining together those that are awakened and training them up in the ways of God, is only begetting children for the murderer. . . .[A]ll over Pembrokeshire . . . nine in ten of the once-awakened are now faster asleep than ever."[9]

For Wesley, this meant preaching in the context of the Lord's Supper and the Anglican catechisms. For present-day Wesleyans, it will look somewhat different, but the point is the same. The preacher's message should be couched and buttressed in the full life and faith of the church. To give people an experience of God, no matter how enlightening, without also revealing the way into the cruciform life is a dangerous handling of the mysteries.

Denominations and individual congregations have sought in a variety of creative ways to teach and nurture people into the centrality of the Word. Several time-honored ways deserve brief attention here.

LECTIONARY AND LITURGICAL CALENDAR

Many today are rediscovering the church's wisdom contained in the gift of its lectionary readings and the Christian liturgical calendar. A lectionary is a book that organizes passages from the Bible, putting them into sets with common themes. Through the history of the church a variety of lectionaries has been used by Orthodox, Roman Catholic, Episcopal, and other Christian traditions.

Usually an attempt is made to balance texts from the Hebrew Scriptures, from the Psalms, from the Epistles, and from the Gospels as a way of qualifying their importance for the church's reflection. In the widely-used *Revised Common Lectionary*, a three-year cycle of lessons for Sunday readings and a two-year cycle for daily readings cover the Bible's teachings in a three-year period. Placing these readings within the broader scope of the Christian calendar not only teaches the congregation the content of the Bible. It also draws them into salvation history, exposed as it is through the weekly liturgical colors, the drama, and the progression of themes throughout the church year.

Besides giving the preacher a scope and sequence for discipleship, the lectionary has another happy outcome. When sitting down to prepare the week's sermon, a set of texts already has been assigned. The proclaimer is as much a receiver of the Word as the congregation who hears it. One of the benefits of following the lectionary readings is that the local congregation is given the counsel of the whole Bible over an extended period of time. The outcome of this should be obvious—a well-balanced diet for ecclesial discipleship; conversely, not to preach from the whole Bible risks turning sermons into lessons on pop psychology, "felt needs," or some other of the preacher's own hobbyhorses. If the pastor chooses to develop such a text system independently, it is imperative to be intentional about the text choices so the Word of God is the determining factor for all that is shaped in, and all that shapes, the local congregation.

From time to time, thematic or book preaching enables other support groups in the local church to build a common conversation around the preacher's text. People can participate in what God is saying because they have been training their ears to hear God's voice. This starts in the formative levels of children's church and continues through all the structures of the church.

> "Whether you like it or not, read and pray daily. It is for your life; there is no other way: else you will be a trifler all your days, and a petty, superficial preacher."
>
> —John Wesley,
> *Letter to John Trembath*

Reciting the Apostles' Creed and the Lord's Prayer, and participating in other symbols that go back to the birth of the Church's faith, are additional ways the local body of Christ can transcend its own parochial setting. When local churches participate in the practices of the Church universal, we are bound by more than mystical communion. Though some fear that adding such formal elements to their church services may destroy the effectual qualities of worship, just the opposite usually proves true. Modern (even postmodern) congregations are showing signs of anemia for lack of concrete and tangible connections with the incarnated faith. Many in the new emergent movement are seeking those deeply rooted symbols in the Celtic and Eastern traditions. Since we have them available to us, why should we not make use of them?

CATECHISMS AND TEACHING

The ancient church learned very early that the experience of Christ needed to be given concrete form in the church's teaching and preaching. They created a Christian "catechism"—a body and process of doctrine—to disciple their converts and children into the faith. They attempted to boil down the basic Christian beliefs into systematic and sensible processes. If modeling clay were the analogy of Christian life, the catechism was the children's toy press that squished out Christians in the pattern of Jesus. Without it, we would be left to play in the dough, even to have a good time, but would have no form or expression of that experience. Good preaching, in the context of the total spiritual formation of the church, makes Christians more like their Master. The entire worship service seeks to get us into the experience, but the sermon itself is the form that gives shape and content to the hour. Too often Christian worship services today are groups of people allowing themselves to be squished and pressed by varying emotions—which may or may not be an enjoyable

> True reconciliation occurs when you confront the demands of the gospel of Jesus Christ with issues of justice and peace, and compassion and caring.
>
> —Desmond Tutu, "Allies of God"

process—but never being shaped by the mind of God. True worship, as Jesus said, is accomplished in Spirit and in truth.

Remembering that the preaching of the sermon is participation with the wider church community, both in worship and in discipleship, we recognize the dynamic character of our sermon preparation. As we design the sermon we are aware of words, themes, and core values that permeate our local church at all levels. At the same time, our final product delivered before the church on the Lord's Day is a prism reflecting and refracting the full-orbed life of the church, both now and into the world without end.

PURPOSE—THE HOPE OF PREACHING

Too many preachers stop the telescoping of the sermon's place at this point—from the preacher's context, to the sermon, and then to the congregation. If they got it, that's enough! The current concern for relevancy becomes the main gauge of success in preaching. However, stopping here dangerously freezes congregational prejudices. To take the indispensable next step of placing the sermon at the center of an even greater dynamic is to understand the role of the transforming Word in moving us toward our purposed end, that is, to participate in God's new creation!

Preaching for transformation is not merely an individualistic goal. To be sure, a sermon that connects with individuals, bringing them in their human condition face-to-face with the Word of God, does bring about life changes. But the wider result is a changed community, even a transformed society. Preaching should not be characterized as someone yelling "Fire!" in a burning building. Vastly more important is therapeutic instruction on how to put the fire out.

When Dr. Martin Luther King Jr. preached from the steps of the Lincoln Memorial to a country torn with racial hatred and injustice, he did more than chastise and judge. He shared a dream, a vision of what The Beloved Community might look like if people took real, practical steps toward that goal. We used to call this prophetic preaching. Today this type of preaching either has been hijacked by political ideologies, both conservative and liberal, or it has been domesticated by those seeking to be sensitive to the unchurched or unconverted. Walter Brueggemann frames the issue squarely:

> The theological scandal of biblical faith, especially when rendered into political, economic issues, is indeed upsetting. How is a pastor to give voice to this scandal in a society that is hostile to it, in a church that is often unwilling to host the scandal, and when we ourselves as teachers and pastors of the church are somewhat queasy about the scandal as it touches our own lives? How can the radical dimension of the Bible as it touches public reality be heard in the church?[10]

I believe the answers are found within the Wesleyan model of grace. Prophetic preaching points the fragile, sinful church to her inheritance in the everlasting reign of God. The preaching event should hold in tension a real and critical picture of the context of the congregation (this present world) together with an equally real picture of the world God is creating. Sermons that are mere utopian dreams of heaven and ideological depictions of love, harmony, and peace offer no real motivation for individual or social transformation. Hope is the ultimate attitude of the preacher who, from the vantage point of the text, sees over the despair of the present world into the Promised Land.

Too often we get hung up on whether to preach God's wrath and judgment or God's love and forgiveness. We need to discover new and old metaphors to retire this needless dichotomy. Preaching should be immersed in grace. As one homiletician has counseled, "Make grace the first and last word, always."[11] Preachers in the Wesleyan spirit understand and value the role of the Holy Spirit in drawing people to that grace. At the same time, this is a transforming grace, prophetically addressing the present with a view to the future.

Many of us preachers today need to discover new ways to prepare for, write, and deliver the Sunday morning sermon. Understanding the fundamental theology behind preaching ensures that preparation for the sermon goes on all week long. In the flow of history and of life, the text places its demands on the congregation as well as on the preacher. From Monday to Sunday the preacher feels that tension. His or her task, finally, is to deliver the sermon responsibly at the center of the worshiping community's life together, the primary weekly worship service(s).

Perhaps one of the main benefits of rediscovering the central role of the sermon, not only in the primary worship service, but also in the center of the church's life and hope, is that a truly lively worship

> How can the radical dimension of the Bible as it touches public reality be heard in the church?
>
> —Walter Brueggemann, "The Preacher, the Text, and the People"

can be rooted again in historic gospel faith. The Word, God's revelation in clarity and content, gives meaning to the Sacrament, the experience of God in our midst. The sermon is freed from becoming a lecture (perhaps garnished with audio-visual wizardry) or being reduced to dramatic entertainment. Notwithstanding even highly effective new technologies for extending the Church into the culture, no substitute exists for building the Church on the foundation of the Christian story in the context of the real world. The plain words, spoken by a well-informed preacher, will point the Church in all her complex struggles to the hope that shapes her future reward.

ACTION SUGGESTIONS

1. Somewhere in the middle of your sermon preparation week, arrange a meeting or call a selected person in your church to discuss the ideas fomenting in your personal Bible study. Choose a different person each week, trying to represent the various age, gender, and social strata of your congregation. Make sure you listen to them, not merely talk to them, and then try to incorporate something of their life and wisdom in the sermon text that Sunday.

2. Commit yourself to reading a literary resource—either contemporary or classic—at least once a month. This literature should come from some source other than traditional evangelical books and print. Allow your congregation to see that you are as literate about the culture you live in as you are about the Bible you preach—and that you are serious about making real life connections between the two.

3. Develop a seminar for the worship leaders of your church to instruct them into a "word-centered" worship experience. Discuss how music, prayer, and congregational involvement impact the preached Word, and vice versa. Together, discover ways to allow the preacher and the sermon a hallowed space in the worship service.

4. Check your preaching schedule for suitable times to engage topics of contemporary/social importance.

FOR FURTHER READING

Bartlett, David Lyon. *Between the Bible and the Church: New Methods for Biblical Preaching.* Nashville: Abingdon Press, 1999.

Dealing with the connection between the preacher's historical-critical study of the Bible and the contemporary, local church setting, Bartlett provides a fairly readable survey of an array of current biblical interpretive methods and explains how they might aid in the preacher's task.

Bonhoeffer, Dietrich. *Worldly Preaching: Lectures on Homiletics.* Edited by Clyde E. Fant. New York: Crossroad, 1991. (Replaces an earlier edition published by Thomas Nelson, 1975.)

Fant's extensive foreword gives a foundational understanding of what it means to preach the Word in the modern context. Bonhoeffer first imparted these seminal ideas to the preachers-in-training of his own homiletics classes at Finkenwalde.

Burghardt, Walter J. *Preaching the Just Word.* New Haven: Yale Univ. Press, 1996.

Included in one of *Newsweek* magazine's "top twelve preachers in America" lists, this Roman Catholic theologian has written an excellent text, seeking to show how biblical preaching informs the ethical teachings of the Church.

Greenhaw, David M. and **Allen**, Ronald J., eds. *Preaching in the Context of Worship.* St. Louis: Chalice Press, 2000.

A collection of essays addressing ways contemporary preachers might build a closer connection between preaching and worship. Ecumenical in nature, this volume treats music in worship, lay preaching, Holy Communion, and other important topics.

Stott, John R. W. *Between Two Worlds: The Art of Preaching in the Twentieth Century.* Grand Rapids: Wm. B. Eerdmans Publishing Co., 1982.

Somewhat dated, but still a good primer in basic evangelical preaching. Stott, in a time of great uncertainty, defends the role of preaching in addressing the struggles of the modern world with the efficacy of the Bible.

NOTES

1. For further reading on Calvin's approach to biblical preaching, see the helpful book by T. H. L Parker, *Calvin's Preaching* (Louisville: Westminster/John Knox Press, 1992).

2. For those with theological interests, this method looks much like that of Don S. Browning, ed., *Practical Theology: The Emerging Field in Theology, Church, and World* (San Francisco: Harper and Row, 1983).

3. John Wesley, March 29, 1739, *The Works of the Rev. John Wesley*, ed. Thomas Jackson, 14 vols., CD-ROM edition (Franklin, TN: Providence House, 1994); 1:85.

4. John Wesley, "A Letter to James Hervey, March 20" (1739), in *The Letters of John Wesley*, ed. John Telford (Epworth Press, 1931).

5. John R. W. Stott, *Between Two Worlds: The Art of Preaching in the Twentieth Century* (Grand Rapids: Wm. B. Eerdmans Publishing Co., 1982), 180.

6. John Wesley, "Letter to John Trembath, August 17" (1760), in *The Letters of John Wesley, Volume 4*, ed. John Telford (Epworth Press, 1931).

7. Clyde E. Fant, *Bonhoeffer: Worldly Preaching* (Nashville: Thomas Nelson, 1975), 18.

8. William Skudlarek, *The Word in Worship: Preaching in a Liturgical Context* (Nashville: Abingdon Press, 1981), 51.

9. John Wesley, August 25, 1763, *The Journal of John Wesley* (Chicago: Moody Press, 1951), 169. For a modern Roman Catholic rendering of this same idea see Yves Congar, O.P., "Sacramental Worship and Preaching," in *The Renewal of Preaching* (Concilium 33; New York: Paulist Press, 1968), 60.

10. Walter Brueggemann, "The Preacher, the Text, and the People," *Theology Today*, vol. 47, no. 3 (Oct., 1990), 237.

11. Rodney J. Hunter, "Preaching Forgiveness in a Therapeutic Age," *Journal for Preachers*, vol. XXVIII, no. 2 (Lent, 2005), 32.

SHAPING UP
THE PREACHER

Credibility

J. Michael Walters

Sanctify them by the truth; your word is truth.

—John 17:17

*I want to know one thing . . . the way to heaven; how to land safe
on that happy shore. God Himself has condescended to show
us the way. He has written it down in a book. Oh, give me
that book! At any price, give me the book of God.*

—John Wesley, *Sermons on Several Occasions*

MEANS OF GRACE

I met Dr. Roy S. Nicholson, one of the church's true Patriarchs, by
coincidence as a college student. He preached one of our school
"revivals," and I was asked to be his chauffeur. I had no idea who he
was, or why it was an honor to cart that old gentleman around, but
what I saw was a man who lived in the Scriptures. The disciplines of
sermon-making were etched deeply into every facet of his life. As a
twenty-year-old aspiring preacher, I thought he was about the most
Christlike person I'd ever met. He certainly treated me as I thought
Jesus would treat others. As I watched him preach that week, and talked
with him in the car, I began to sense something of the transformational

nature of preaching. Preaching is an invitation to God to finish what He started when we were born anew into the Kingdom.

I wonder, as I sometimes hear pastors complain about the weekly pressure to "come up with another sermon," whether they grasp the opportunity they have to go deep with God in and through their preaching ministries. The ministry is not just about what we are called to do *for* God, it also is the means by which God would do something *to* us.

No preacher can give him or herself to the weekly regimens of preparing to preach without being profoundly changed, indeed transformed, by the double-edged sword of God's Word. Any preacher who consistently wrestles with Scripture has taken perhaps the most important step in becoming an embodiment of the authority and inspiration of the Bible.

Henri Nouwen has said, "Often the most important result in preaching is the conversion of the preacher!" For those who have given years of their lives to the preaching task, Nouwen's words are a reminder of how profoundly this task has changed us, for the good. For those just starting in ministry, Nouwen's words are filled with anticipation of God's using the tasks of ministry to continue to perfect His saving intentions in us.

STUDY

Preaching is the hardest, most exacting work I have ever undertaken. Only those who have learned how to replenish the spiritual well can stay at it for long at a level approximating excellence. This is why preachers need not expend great effort trying to maintain strict lines between preaching and our own devotional lives. I'm not sure it would be a good thing even if we could manage it. In spite of all that has been written about the dangers of using devotional times for sermon-making, I'm convinced that the greater problem is the failure to keep God and our pursuit of God at the center of our sermon-making. It has often been in the midst of seeking God's word for my congregation that I have heard most clearly God's word for my own life as well. Fred Craddock's question is well taken: "What minister has not experienced a desk becoming an altar?"[1]

God uses ministry to form ministers spiritually. The task of sermon preparation represents the optimum time for God to work on us however He wills. That's why ministers never need to apologize for their study time. Indeed, to quote Craddock again, "Time spent in study is never *getting away* from daily work but *getting into* daily work. The hours of study bear directly and immediately both on who the minister is and on the minister's influence by word and action. It is in the study that so much of the minister's formation of character and faith takes place."[2] The classic rhetoricians insisted that powerful and effective preaching both originates and flourishes in the formation of that character and faith.

> If a preacher is not first preaching to himself, better that he falls on the steps of the pulpit and breaks his neck than preaches that sermon.
>
> —John Calvin, cited in Rowell, *Preaching with Spiritual Passion*

Our personal engagement with Scripture is the necessary starting point, both for our own spiritual growth and for that of our congregations. Underscoring the importance of preachers personally engaging with the Word, John Calvin said, "If a preacher is not first preaching to himself, better that he falls on the steps of the pulpit and breaks his neck than preaches that sermon."[3] I've heard enough sermons to believe that some nimble-footed preachers manage to ascend their pulpits, Calvin's warning notwithstanding.

We are ultimately revealed for who we truly are. Lazy preachers inevitably get found out. This typically comes at the point of the shallowness of their own spiritual and intellectual development. No

> No amount of technical exegetical skill compensates for a failure to attend to Scripture as the living word of God. The pastor's exegetical task is in service to the aliveness of this word. Exegesis, if it is to serve the church's life and be congruent to the pastor's calling, must be contemplative exegesis.
>
> —Eugene Peterson,
> *Working the Angles: The Shape of Pastoral Integrity*

preacher who hesitates to pay the price in the study ought to be optimistic about the long-term fruitfulness of a ministry. When the hard work of sermon preparation is neglected, the ministry is fundamentally malnourished. This is why study is a nonnegotiable spiritual discipline for preachers. Perhaps no human will ever know the time we spend preparing, but God's approval is what matters. When the Apostle Paul tells Timothy, "Do your best to present yourself to God as one approved, a workman who does not need to be ashamed, and who correctly handles the word of truth" (2 Timothy 2:15), he reminds all of us who handle the Word that we seek the approval of One who knows full well the effort we have expended, the sacrifices we have made.

CONTEMPLATIVE EXEGESIS

Exercising spiritual disciplines fosters the depth necessary to be effective in the pulpit for the long term. One practice fundamental to shaping the preacher is meditation. Many lay Christians benefit regularly from the discipline of engaging Scripture meditatively, but this practice is absolutely crucial in shaping preachers spiritually and in unleashing their full potential in the pulpit. Being in Scripture, listening to God speak to *us* through it, is of paramount importance in cultivating our lives toward effective preaching. We will ever be tempted to use the Bible as a springboard into what *we* want to say; the way to overcome this is to cultivate a deep sensitivity to Scripture—that means spending time with it in study and meditation.

When I speak of "engaging scripture meditatively," I have in mind a sort of homiletical combination of the disciplines of study and meditation, presupposing a healthy practice of solitude, silence, and prayer. Scripture has always played a huge role in ascetical theology, that branch of theology that focuses on our spiritual growth. Wesley termed reading Scripture a "means of grace." Our interest in the Bible is first and foremost in "hearing God speak, not in analyzing moral memos"[4]—nor in finding a text upon which we can hang our Sunday remarks.

I long have believed in and practiced what some term "rumination" in preaching—prayerfully and meditatively immersing oneself into the text early in the week and allowing it to "simmer" on the back burner of our hearts and minds as we go about our days. The church has long advocated this for its preachers. Eugene Peterson observed, "No amount of technical exegetical skill compensates for a failure to attend to Scripture as the living word of God. The pastor's exegetical task is in service to the aliveness of this word. Exegesis, if it is to serve the church's life and be congruent to the pastor's calling, must be *contemplative exegesis*."[5]

I love that term. Contemplative exegesis means taking the Bible seriously *and* taking the time to take the Bible seriously. The leisurely, unhurried aspect that defines this practice can be maintained only through inviolable ministerial priorities. Some preachers may actually need to schedule appointments simply to be alone with God and His word.

Be forewarned: habitually spending time with God changes a person. Willimon quotes Luther as saying of the Bible, "Here is a word that first kills in order to make alive, that damns in order to bless. Preaching is something akin to surgery."[6] Allowing the Bible to have that kind of power in our preaching is necessarily preceded by allowing the Bible to have that kind of power in our own lives.

Marva Dawn has observed, "The greatest weakness in much preaching is that the Word hasn't killed the pastor first!"[7]

Scripture is the medium we use to communicate the revelation of God to others. We live and minister in an age of information overload. People are often tired of processing information when they walk into church. However, we are not in the information business—we are in the revelation business. If we are to prevent our listeners from treating revelation as mere information, we ourselves first must treat it as revelation.

BORN-AGAIN SERMONS

The effectiveness of preachers is determined by the time they spend in preparing both themselves and their sermons. Putting words on paper for the following Sunday is the bare minimum of a preacher's task. As Nouwen reminds us, it's about the "conversion of the preacher"—and converted preachers are absolutely necessary to the health of the church and to the ongoing health of preaching.

> The greatest weakness in much preaching is that the Word hasn't killed the pastor first!
>
> —Marva Dawn, *Reaching out without Dumbing Down*

Putting a premium upon the spiritual depth of the preacher is in stark contrast to much of modern ministry that seems mostly concerned with demonstrating one's relevance to the current culture. Allowing our preaching to proceed from the question posed by Willimon, "What is God using the Bible to do to us?"[8] radically differs from "felt-need" preaching which panders to the trends. I want to see and hear preachers who themselves have been deeply affected by the word they put before the congregation.

To watch the power of Scripture in the life of a preacher is to hear the sermon twice. (By the way, preaching a text that has turned the preacher inside out through the week is a sure antidote to boring sermons.) Willimon notes that John Calvin spoke of sermons being "twice-born," once in the study, then again in the pulpit. He said, "In the pulpit the preacher attempts to recapitulate before the congregation the process of discovery, the surprise and delights of revelation, which the preacher experienced in the study."[9] Born-again sermons can be the products only of born-again preachers, of those preachers who give themselves wholeheartedly and continually to the cultivation of their own souls in submission to the Word of God.

PERSONAL CREDIBILITY

In an age where the Bible's authority is often questioned and lampooned, Willimon notes that we don't need to "trot out our little arguments, but rather our little lives. The truthfulness of scripture is in the lives it is able to produce."[10] Incarnating the Scripture into human life is the ultimate defense of the Bible.

Being powerful advocates for God in the pulpit will never happen by accident. Powerful and effective preaching is the overflow of an increasingly deeper walk with God, intentionally cultivated. This is what makes the preacher's own faith journey so critical. Fred Craddock has written that

the way to communicate the Christian faith is through disciplined participation in that faith. Appropriation of the gospel is the minimum condition for approaching the pulpit or podium. From the standpoint of the hearers, the qualities of the teller affect the response to the story. The decision that a message is worth listening to is a decision that the teller is worth listening to.[11]

> The work of communicating the gospel with the congregation on a weekly basis is too intellectually and spiritually demanding to attempt to do it without regular contact with the wellsprings of inspiration that keep us alive as preachers.
>
> —William Willimon,
> *Pastor: The Theology and Practice of Ordained Ministry*

Craddock is saying that modern preachers require personal credibility—but in truth that always has been the case. Jesus' teaching was immediately judged as being different from that of the Scribes and Pharisees by virtue of what Matthew termed "authority" (Matt. 7:28–29). That kind of authority emerges from the depths of one's relationship with the Father.

The ancient Greeks, who developed the science of rhetoric, knew three crucial components comprise persuasive speech. These are *logos*, *pathos*, and *ethos*—what is said, how it is said, and who says it. From Aristotle through Augustine, not one person disputed the claim that *ethos*, the character of the speaker, is the most important element of public speaking.

Modern preachers also know that their own spiritual lives, demonstrably shaped by the word they preach to others, will be the most crucial factor in their effectiveness in the pulpit. Believability, authenticity, and unmistakable spirituality confirm and lend authority to the preached word.

The current "image-making culture" is devastating to the ministry. Ed Rowell has observed, "Nothing is easier to caricature than a preacher, and nothing is harder to build than the character of a preacher. No wonder some preachers go for style over substance."[12] Building the life of spiritual character—by virtue of the fact that it doesn't come easily or quickly—flies in the face of our image-is-everything world.

Real depth in preaching results from those aspects of our lives which are below the waterline—where no one sees but ourselves and

God. To give ourselves intentionally to the task of building those dimensions of our lives that no one really sees is difficult and goes to the heart of one's commitment to be a thoroughly furnished servant of God. But the necessity of this pursuit for anyone who would preach with authority and power is beyond argument. William Willimon correctly notes, "The work of communicating the gospel with the congregation on a weekly basis is too intellectually and spiritually demanding to attempt to do it without regular contact with the wellsprings of inspiration that keep us alive as preachers."[13]

PREACHERETTES

Commenting on the plight of preaching in the modern church, John Stott observed that "ours is the age of the sermonette, and sermonettes produce Christianettes."[14] Abounding evidence underscores the legitimacy of Stott's concern. I have come to suspect that sermonettes produce preacherettes, as well. The diminishing of preaching not only shrinks the church; it shrinks the church's preachers. God cannot fully develop any preacher into the person He envisions if that person is satisfied with delivering the sentimental little ditties that too often pass for sermons these days. Healthy, robust diets are required not only for those in the pews, but

> Ours is the age of the sermonette, and sermonettes produce Christianettes.
>
> —John Stott,
> *Between Two Worlds*

also (especially) for those who endeavor to feed Jesus' sheep. To starve to death on one's own cooking would be the greatest tragedy in a minister's life.

With so many church leaders reducing themselves to preacherettes, the church is suffering disastrous long-term effects. The importance of the preaching office has diminished, taking a toll on all ministers, forcing us to find other ways (as counselors, leaders, community spokespersons, etc.) to demonstrate our significance to the church.

Even so, there is no more important task for any minister than to stand before his or her flock and proclaim God's Word, backed up by a life that incarnates the Word proclaimed. No sermon subscription service, no video-conferencing of celebrity speakers, no high-energy sermon work group can suffice for a man or woman who has waited upon, wrestled with, and prayed to God for an appropriate word for their flock each Sunday. It's the difference between having a home-cooked Thanksgiving dinner and buying one of those ready-made "feasts" at the supermarket. The food may look identical and contain similar ingredients, but it's just not the same, and everyone sitting around the table knows it. Most of all, the "cook" knows it.

ACT OF WORSHIP

Another way the preaching ministry fosters the preacher's own spiritual formation is the way it affects his or her personal worship. As I began to consider how God used preaching to work in my personal spiritual development, I realized how preaching became part of my experience in corporate worship as well. The congregation gathers to worship, bringing offerings of praises, prayers, songs, and tithes to the Most High God. But for preachers, the sermon itself becomes part of the way *we* worship God.

In a moment of epiphany, I began to see my sermon, including all its preparation, as an offering. When I submitted to God what I had painstakingly crafted—not only for Him to use in the hearts and lives of the congregation, but as an expression of my love for God— I gained a new and deeper respect for the preaching office which energized my own worship. If soloists can offer up beautiful pieces of music as expressions of adoration in acceptance of God's gifts, why can't preachers offer up the sermon in similar fashion? We not only can, but we should. Not only is preaching an expression of our love and care for God's people, it is also an expression of our love for God himself.

Only those pastors who intentionally choose the ministerial road increasingly less-traveled will be able to avoid the pressures to compromise their preaching. Eugene Peterson has written powerfully about the necessity of maintaining one's sense of pastoral vocation in the middle of a community of people who hire us to do religious jobs. And, perhaps we've decided that doing "religious jobs" is preferable.

> Nothing is easier to caricature than a preacher, and nothing is harder to build than the character of a preacher. No wonder some preachers go for style over substance.
>
> —Ed Rowell, *Preaching with Spiritual Passion*

As Peterson puts it, "The answer [to a pastor's vocational work] among the masters whom I consult doesn't change: a trained attentiveness to God in prayer, in Scripture reading, in spiritual direction. This has not been tried and discarded because it didn't work, but tried and found difficult (and more than a little bit tedious) and so shelved in favor of something or other that could be fit into a busy pastor's schedule. . . . The fact is that nobody has an aptitude for it. It is hard work. It is unglamorous work."[15] Nothing is more central to the pastoral vocation than speaking to the people on God's behalf.

I look back now on my years of preaching weekly and see them as the most important years of my life in my own spiritual growth. Admittedly, I don't exactly know all that happened during those eighteen years of pastoral preaching except for this: the preacher got converted. I'm beginning to think that's not bad at all.

ACTION SUGGESTIONS

1. Schedule blocks of time (minimum of 45 minutes) to read repeatedly and meditate on (think about prayerfully) a particular text of Scripture. Jot down things that come to mind, even if you think them insignificant. They may not be.

2. Practice using your imagination when you work with Scripture. Put yourself into the situation of the text or the mood of the psalmist, for example. Get used to identifying with the realities of the text.

3. Get in the habit of putting your Sunday text into your mind as early in the week as possible. Work with it enough on Monday, for example, so that it's ruminating in the background of your mind and you can connect things that happen and things you read to the text throughout the week.

4. Use your sermon preparation as a time when God can speak to you personally through His word. Try to answer the question, "What may God want to say to *me* through this text?" What application(s) can you make in your own life?

FOR FURTHER READING

Peterson, Eugene H. *Working the Angles: The Shape of Pastoral Integrity*. Grand Rapids: Wm. B. Eerdmans Publishing Co., 1987.

No one holds pastors ruthlessly accountable to their true vocation like Eugene Peterson. This book has been a chart and compass for me from the day it was published.

Rowell, Ed. *Preaching with Spiritual Passion: How to Stay Fresh in Your Calling*. Minneapolis: Bethany House, 1998.

Ed Rowell knows that preaching is more than preparing sermons; it's also preparing preachers. He knows the "insides" of preachers; hence, he knows how to talk our language.

Willimon, William H. *Pastor: The Theology and Practice of Ordained Ministry*. Nashville: Abingdon Press, 2002.

No one else has shaped my understanding of the pastoral vocation as deeply as has Will Willimon. His grasp of Scripture and theology in defining the role of pastor and preacher demonstrates why this is the greatest vocation in the world.

NOTES

1. Fred Craddock, *Preaching* (Nashville: Abingdon Press, 1985), 70.
2. Ibid.
3. Ed Rowell, *Preaching with Spiritual Passion*, (Minneapolis: Bethany House, 1998), 89.
4. Fred Craddock, *Overhearing the Gospel* (Nashville: Abingdon, 1978), 43.
5. Fred Craddock, *Preaching* (Nashville: Abingdon, 1985), 70.
6. Ibid.
7. Marva Dawn, *Reaching out without Dumbing Down* (Grand Rapids, Wm. B. Eerdmans Publishing Co., 1995), 219.
8. Willimon, op. cit., 113.
9. Ibid., 148.
10. Ibid., 130.
11. Fred Craddock, *Overhearing the Gospel* (Nashville: Abingdon Press, 1978), 43.
12. Rowell, op. cit., 109.
13. Willimon, op. cit., 155.
14. John R.W. Stott, *Between Two Worlds* (Grand Rapids: Wm. B. Eerdmans Publishing Co., 1982), 7.
15. Eugene Peterson, *Working the Angles: The Shape of Pastoral Integrity* (Grand Rapids: Wm. B. Eerdmans Publishing Co., 1987), 11.

THE TABLE
OF INSPIRATION

Interpreting the Bible

Ken Schenck

*Do your best to present yourself to God as one approved, a workman who
does not need to be ashamed and who correctly handles the word of truth.*

—2 Timothy 2:15

*If, then, we have spoken the word of God . . . and that only; if we have
put no unnatural interpretation upon it, but taken the known phrases
in their common obvious sense,—and when they were less known,
explained scripture by scripture; if we have spoken the whole word
as occasion offered . . . —then, believe ye our works if not our words;
or rather, believe them both together. Here is all a Preacher can do.*

—John Wesley, Sermon CXXXVI, "On Corrupting the Word of God"

THE TIGHT ROPE OF BIBLE STUDY

The professor was emphasizing the difference between reading
the words of the Bible in their original context and just reading
them as they strike you. A rather energetic student immediately
voiced a concern. "The thing is," he said, "a lot of seniors come
through their Bible classes with a sense of defeat. 'I could never have
come up with that professor's interpretation,' some say. Some of them
have pretty much decided not to use the Bible in their preaching." The
professor was aghast. Talk about unintended outcomes!

Training in how to interpret and preach from the Bible is like walking a tight rope. On the one hand, surely we should be interested in what the words of the Bible actually meant to those to whom they were first written. Yet we also want the Bible to speak as God's living and relevant word to our congregations. On the one side we run the risk of getting bogged down in highly technical method and study. The Bible can become like a dissected frog whose parts we know, but that is dead. On the other side we run the risk of generating relevant sermons that are simply mirrors of our culture and what we think, but not a challenging word from God.

On the whole, we probably tend to err more on the side of relevance today than on the side of over-attention to the original meaning. For that reason, this chapter focuses on the kinds of things we need to consider when we are targeting what Isaiah or Paul or John actually meant originally when God inspired them to write to their particular audiences. Sound exegesis and study in sermon preparation give depth to our sermons. Without such foundations, our sermons can be entertaining houses of straw that blow away as quickly as they are uttered. Without depth, our sermons can be houses built on sand that fall flat with the rain. True, God can speak through us even if we do not know the original meaning. But surely our preaching will only gain in power if this meaning is a significant part of the sermon equation.

THAT WAS THEN

Taking the words of Scripture and applying them directly to oneself is a natural tendency. Countless Christians have heard God's voice through the Bible in this way. However, a little reflection makes it clear that to read the Bible this way is to read the words differently from what they originally meant. Ironically, some of those who are most emphatic about taking the Bible literally do not notice that the Bible literally tells us its books were written to someone else.

Romans says it was written to (mid-first-century) Christians in Rome (Rom. 1:7). Isaiah's visions concerned the Judah and Jerusalem of the eighth century before Christ (Is. 1:1). Even Revelation says it is about things that will "soon take place" (Rev. 1:1), and its direct addressees were seven churches in late first-century Asia Minor (Rev. 1:4). My point is not to dismiss the sacramental use of Scripture that immediately hears God's voice in the words. It is to qualify this use of the Bible by noting that when we read the words this way, we are not reading them as they were first intended to be read.

The original audiences did not bring a twenty-first-century American view of the world to bear on the words. Thinking God spoke over the heads of these audiences so the words would be just right for me is an inadvertent yet massive narcissism. Who am I? Am I better or more sophisticated than they were? If the words work that way, maybe they actually target my great-grandchildren rather than me?

Many Christians have heard God's voice from the story of God commanding Abraham to sacrifice Isaac. A. W. Tozer found in this story the need to surrender everything to God, even the thing most precious to you.[1] Some Christian philosophers have used this story to argue that God is the one who defines morality and that if God commands murder, then murder is good in that instance. Søren Kierkegaard saw in this story an example of the incomprehensibility of God, His paradoxical nature that is beyond understanding.[2]

It may be that these Christian voices have seen truths in this story. However, we cannot understand the *original* meaning of this story unless we know something about child sacrifice in the ancient world. The horrific world in which fathers sometimes sacrificed their children to appease the gods was an ancient memory even by the time of the New Testament, let alone in our time. Consider the Moabite king who sacrificed his firstborn son on top of the walls of his city to curry favor with his god against Israel (2 Kings 3:26–27). Read against such horrific practices, Abraham's story was originally a powerful statement that God was not like the gods others served back then. God does not require human sacrifice (cf. Lev. 18:21). We will understand this meaning only if we know something of the world in which Genesis was written and in which Abraham lived.

The actions God commanded at other times and places will frequently not have the same meaning or consequences if we do them today. I can greet the brothers in my church with a kiss as Paul instructed the Thessalonians (1 Thess. 5:26), but it will not do the same thing it did two thousand years ago. A holy handshake will suffice today. Considering oneself the immediate audience of the Bible's words holds a latent danger. Sometimes doing exactly what God commanded someone else can have a result the opposite of what God wants one to do today.

For example, Deuteronomy 21:15–17 gives instructions to a man with two wives. These instructions presume that it is perfectly normal for a husband to have more than one wife. Indeed, Mormons and various other cults have used Old Testament passages like these to justify polygamy. But God would not want any Christian to have more than one spouse today. Not only does the New Testament operate on this assumption (e.g., 1 Cor. 7:2), but this is the position of the church of the ages. Both Jesus and Paul model a use of Scripture that applies the heart of biblical commands, more than a slavishly literal or direct application. It was more those who opposed them who insisted on applying the words directly and absolutely to what was, even then, a quite different world from Old Testament times.

Before we can really listen to what God inspired the ancient authors to write, we must be clear who the ancient audience was. We will scarcely apply the words correctly to today if we know only what God said but not why he said it. The first step in reading the Bible's words for meaning today is to know what they originally meant.

THE TREES AND THE FOREST

Reading Scripture in so much detail that we miss the big picture, the overall context in which the words are located, results in a skewed understanding of the original meaning. On the other hand, we can also skew our overall picture of a text's meaning because we have not taken the details into account, appropriately.

THE BIG PICTURE

Careful observation of the big picture requires us to take the literary context of a particular verse or passage into account. Have we simply read a verse in isolation from the other verses around it? Much Christian use of the Bible through the centuries has pushed us toward seeing individual verses in isolation. Evangelicals and fundamentalists are to be commended for teaching their children memory verses; but the danger in this practice is programming our children to see individual statements as timeless truths without teaching them how to understand those statements in the light of their contexts. English versions of the Bible that present each verse as a self-standing statement, such as the King James Version, encourage this tendency.

We will not correctly understand the original meaning of an individual verse unless we read the words before and after it. As an example, take Hosea's statement, "Out of Egypt I called my son." The immediate context provides the original meaning: "When Israel was a child, I loved him, and *out of Egypt I called my son*. But the more I called Israel, the further they went from me. They sacrificed to the Baals and they burned incense to images (Hosea 11:1–2, emphasis added)." We read this sequence of words from Hosea in context when we read them in light of the words that come immediately before and after them.

Ironically, Matthew himself gives us a good illustration of what it is like to read these words *out of context*. He applied these same words—"out of Egypt I called my son"—to the departure of Jesus' family from Egypt. Matthew reported that Joseph "got up, took the child and his mother during the night and left for Egypt, where he stayed until the death of Herod. And so was fulfilled what the Lord had said through the prophet: 'Out of Egypt I called my son'" (Matt. 2:14–15). From the immediate literary context of these words in Hosea, the original meaning referred to Israel and its exodus from Egypt rather than to Jesus. Matthew reads them out of their original context and against the context of Jesus' early life. I use this example to strike a healthy balance in interpretation. We should try to know the original context. After all, it shows respect to Hosea! Yet apparently God is not bound by the confines of the original meaning. The Bible is a sacrament from which God can speak regardless of how well we understand the original meaning.

Youth pastors for years have used 2 Corinthians 6:14–7:1 ("Do not be yoked together with unbelievers. . .") as a preaching text to urge Christian teens not to date non-Christians. Yet these verses were not originally about dating or even about marriage to unbelievers.[3] The broader literary context suggests that the main reason the Corinthians were "withholding affection" from Paul was because of their association with unbelievers (6:13). The point of the original meaning is similar to the way this text is often used in preaching, but is not quite the same. Good preachers will be aware of these subtle differences.

Part of looking at the big picture is knowing the genre of the book you are interpreting. We would not expect books like Acts or 2 Kings to conform to the way we write history books today. Why would they, when they were first written to ancient audiences? We would expect them to look more like ancient histories. Similarly, we should not be surprised if a Gospel would exhibit similarities to an ancient biography. The more serious we are about finding the original meaning, the more we will try to learn about how the genre (e.g., ancient letters, apocalyptic literature, wisdom literature, etc.) was created and understood.

The literary context of these books may or may not go beyond the individual books themselves.[4] For example, Matthew is ultimately not part of the literary context of Exodus or Romans. The sacramental use of Scripture tends to read the Bible as a single book from God to me (and God does speak to people in this way repeatedly); but each book of the Bible uses words in its own way on its own terms. Thus we will not gain too much illumination of the original meaning of Hebrews by recourse to Luke. Differentiating between books in the canon is a fundamental aspect of reading in context, but it goes against the grain of the idea of interpreting Scripture with Scripture, as is so often done today. We do *weigh* scripture against scripture, but we usually cannot interpret the precise original meaning of one part of Scripture with that of another.

Revelation 22:18–19 originally applied to the book of Revelation alone, "I warn everyone who hears the words of the prophecy of this book: If anyone adds anything to them, God will add to him the plagues described in this book. And if anyone takes words away from this book of prophecy, God will take away from him his share in the tree of life and in the holy city, which are described in this book." Perhaps these words *spiritually* apply to the whole Bible today since the passage appears at the end of the Bible. But the original meaning of these words came at a time when the individual books of the Bible circulated independently on their own individual scrolls. The original meaning of these verses related only to the book of Revelation.

THE DETAILS

If there is a danger of focusing so much on the details that we miss the broader context, it is also possible to miss out on the broader meaning because we do not pay enough attention to the details.

Ultimately, such attention to detail requires the ability to work in Greek, Hebrew, and Aramaic, the original languages of the books of the Bible. Knowing these languages will not answer all questions about the meaning of a verse or passage. But no hope exists of precisely understanding the original meaning without knowing these languages. Using multiple translations and good commentaries does at least get us in the ballpark, however, if we do not have access to the original languages.

An example of neglecting both the details of the verse itself and the broader literary and historical context can be found in the interpretation of 1 John 1:8: "If we claim to be without sin, we deceive ourselves and the truth is not in us." This verse long has served as a proof text to argue that Christians cannot help but sin their whole lives. The detail it misses is the exact meaning. The text does not say, "If we claim that we do not sin." The text says, "If we say that we do not *have* sin" (author's translation). The first wording would imply that we continue to sin as Christians. But the more precise translation means only that all have sinned. The broader context it neglects is that John does not see sin as the norm of a Christian's life (see 1 John 3:9).[5]

When the questions we ask of the biblical text relate closely to good observations of the biblical text, we are on the road to good interpretation and the original meaning. For example, when reading Jeremiah 1:5 ("Before I formed you in the womb I knew you, before you were born I set you apart; I appointed you a prophet to the nations."), the question "What does this verse say about abortion?" is not a good original-meaning question, for this passage does not address the issue of abortion. The path to the original meaning would be a question like, "Who is speaking and who is being spoken to?"

Other good questions are, "What did God mean when He said He formed Jeremiah in his mother's womb?" "How literal is this statement?" "What was the worldview of Judeans in Jeremiah's time regarding how babies were formed in the womb?" Such questions are relevant to the original meaning. Perhaps they may help in discerning God's will toward issues like abortion today, but the original meaning did not address that question.

INTERPRETING WITH INTEGRITY

We now move from what the text says to what it means. A valuable tool in this process is the word study. A word or phrase study is an examination of the various ways a word or phrase was used in a particular culture and especially by a particular author. We study how an author used a word or phrase elsewhere in the book we are studying, then in any other books by that author, then in the books of the Testament in which the book is found, then in the other Testament, then in the secular literature of the language from which the word comes. Finally, we return to the verse we started with and bring this information to determine what the word or phrase means in the context we are interpreting.

This is quite a task. To do it exhaustively will be beyond both the time constraints and the resources of almost all preachers. A fortunate preacher might be able to exhaust the Bible if she has the appropriate resources at hand.[6] Beyond the Bible, the preacher usually will have to rely on theological dictionaries, Bible handbooks, and especially on good original-language commentaries for historical background.

Here a good deal of caution is in order. Many older, more popular resources are not only unhelpful; they can be misleading. Some helpful commentary series for a pastor are Eerdmans' New International Commentary series on both the Old and New Testaments, the Interpretation series, and the New International Version Application Bible series. The Wesleyan Publishing House has now almost completed a commentary series from a Wesleyan perspective, and Nazarene Publishing House, as part of the Nazarene centenary, is also launching a new commentary series. These, and some other series, are written from a conservative (some even from a Wesleyan) perspective by scholars equipped to read the Bible in context, in the original languages. Sources like these offer background knowledge one simply would not have otherwise.

It seems worthwhile to mention some of the more prominent mistakes pastors make from pulpits when they are interpreting the Bible's words. Because of the importance we assign to the words of the Bible, all too often we find ourselves interpreting its words out of focus, even in strange and bizarre ways. For example, no one would try to understand the word "understand" by breaking it into its parts, "under" plus "stand." Do I "stand under" a concept when I understand it? Similarly, splitting a Greek word does not necessarily reveal its meaning.

A prominent example of this "etymological" fallacy is the assertion that the church consists of the "called out" ones because the Greek word for church is composed of *ek* plus *kaleo*. In reality, this word had been in ordinary use for centuries before the New Testament, and no one analyzed the word when they used it any more than we do when we use the word *understand*. Acts 19:41 uses this word of the mob the city clerk at Ephesus sent away after their riot—certainly not a group of elect, "called out" ones. Breaking the word apart makes a good sermon illustration, and I am not opposed to using it. But we should present it as an illustration, not as a part of the original meaning.

Similarly, words do not carry every possible nuance they can have every place they are used. Words have a range of possible meanings; but only one, or at most, two are used at any one time. Perhaps the greatest word fallacy interpreters of the Bible use is the "overload" fallacy, where they simply read way too much meaning into a single instance where a word is used. A student once asked if they might do a word study on the word *impossible*, to see what it might mean when Hebrews 6:18 says it is impossible for God to lie. I suggested at the end of the study—if done correctly—the student would only find out that the word means "not possible." It is the *context* of Hebrews 6:18 that gives richness to it, not magical meanings we can overload into the word *impossible* from other contexts where the same word is used. The opposite problem is the "one meaning" fallacy. If a Bible translator boasted that she translated the same word the same way every time it was used, she would be boasting about a poor translation. Language is fluid; it cannot be treated in the rigid way some interpreters treat it.

Another example of reading too much meaning into words is the sharp distinction many Christians make between two Greek words for love, *agapao* and *phileo*. John 21 often is viewed as making such a distinction in Jesus' discussion with Peter, and it may. But this conclusion is far from certain. For example, it is worth noting that the Greek translation of the Old Testament uses *agapao* of the way Amnon felt about Tamar before he raped and discarded her (2 Sam. 13:4). In this instance, *agapao* is far from some heavenly love that pertains only to Christians.

Another word fallacy we find from time to time is the "anachronistic" fallacy, by which a person interprets a word in the light of meanings the word took on only later or from words in other languages that derive from it. Thus, the Greek word *martyr* looks like the English word martyr, but it did not connote a person who witnessed to Christ by death. At that time, it simply meant a witness. Only later did it take on the meaning we give it today.

Just because the root of the word "to baptize" (*baptizo*) means "to dip" (*bapto*) does not indicate that baptism always meant immersion. This is an example of the "root" fallacy (related to the etymological fallacy). Historical evidence reveals that the early Christians probably did usually immerse those they baptized. But the primary meaning of the word can also be "to wash" (e.g., Mark 7:4).

These are just some of the mistakes in using words that pastors (and scholars) sometimes make. But we do not necessarily have to abandon some of them as *illustrations* of meaning (rather than the actual meaning). Congregations often find these kinds of illustrations helpful. We will only want to preface our comments with some statement like, "Now Paul would not have thought of it this way, but notice that the word for *church* here is *ekklesia* . . ."

THE TABLE OF INSPIRATION

A preacher who brings the original meaning to the table of sermon preparation has more to offer the congregation than someone who does not. How could it be otherwise? The original meaning is not the only voice that should speak through the preacher, but it is the starting point of revelation.

Without the Holy Spirit, the most exegetically correct sermon still will be dead. Without the impact of the Spirit as He has spoken through the text and is speaking through the text, we run the risk of presenting our congregations with a dissected frog. We have labeled all the parts, but the frog is dead. Excellent biblical preaching is the wedding of Spirit with depth of insight.

The most crucial element behind a sermon is the presence of the Holy Spirit speaking through the preacher. When the preacher prepares to bring God's word for the day to a congregation, he or she must come to the table of inspiration where God's will is discerned. If we rely only on our own understanding of the Bible, we create the danger of misspeaking for God. If we pretend we do not need the Spirit in addition to the Bible, we run the risk of smuggling our own voice in place of God's. If that happens, God will have to speak around us rather than through us.

We must bring the church, the community of the saints of all the ages, with us to the occasion of preaching. If the Spirit of God inhabits the body of Christ, then we are most likely to hear God's voice when we are in continuity with the community of saints throughout the ages. The weightiest voices of the church are those of the inspired authors of the Bible. Theirs were the foundational moments of revelation, the inspired commencement of the words of the Bible as a sacrament of revelation. More than the spiritual inspiration of a moment, the original meaning of these words gives us the foundational inspiration at the beginning of the final age.

The original meaning of the Bible is the foundation, because it is the bedrock of inspiration. Yet because the original meaning was written to ancient audiences, it does not tell us itself how to incarnate it and apply it to today. For this task we need the assistance of the Holy Spirit, particularly as He has spoken and continues to speak in the church. When we bring these voices to the table of inspiration, God's word will be heard.

ACTION SUGGESTIONS

1. Make a copy of the text from which you plan to preach (more than a week ahead of time, if you can). Begin making observations about that text. Circle key words you think make the main points. Underline prepositions and other "transition" words that seem important to understanding what the text is really saying. Use these observations to shape the main points of your sermon.

2. Pick a key word from your sermon passage that is not completely clear to you. Using a concordance (preferably one keyed to the Greek or Hebrew; try www.blueletterbible.org if you do not have access to one), look up all the places where the book's author uses that word. Look the other passages up to see if they shed light on what that author is saying in your preaching text.

3. When you have done the preceding study, look at three commentaries to see if you have missed anything. Don't be afraid to use your own observations to "critique" the commentaries. How well has each commentary listened to the text?

FOR FURTHER READING

Duvall, J. Scott and Hays, J. Daniel. *Grasping God's Word: A Hands-On Approach to Reading, Interpreting, and Applying the Bible.* Grand Rapids: Zondervan, 2005.

This book is an excellent and detailed explanation of the process of good observation, good interpretation and good application. It includes exceptionally practical tools for how to do word studies, observe the features of a text, and other vital exegetical/hermeneutical tasks.

Marshall, I. Howard. *Beyond the Bible: Moving from Scripture to Theology.* Grand Rapids: Baker Book House, 2004.

This hermeneutical work from an eminent evangelical scholar points to the future of evangelical scholarship on the Bible. In this book Marshall wrestles with the process of appropriating the exegesis of the Bible for our thinking today.

Schenck, Ken. *A Brief Guide to Biblical Hermeneutics.* Marion: Triangle Publishing, 2005.

This short booklet challenges the reader to read the words of the Bible truly in context and thus to appropriate its teaching with integrity for today. It is a more reflective and challenging version of the material in this chapter.

Thompson, David L. *Bible Study That Works.* Nappanee: Evangel Publishing House, 1994.

In a more general way than his mentor (Robert Traina, *Methodical Bible Study*), Thompson sketches the contours of the classic "English Bible" method used at Asbury Theological

Seminary, and leads the reader through the process, from observation to interpretation, evaluation, and appropriation.

NOTES

1. A. W. Tozer, *The Pursuit of God* (Camp Hill, PA: Christian Publications, 1982 [1949]), 21–30.

2. Søren Kierkegaard, *Fear and Trembling*, trans. Walter Lowrie (Princeton: Princeton University Press, 1974 [1843]).

3. Some scholars think these verses originally may have been in a separate letter from Paul to the Corinthians since they seem quite out of place in their immediate context.

4. Of course when we have more than one book by the same author, we can gain very helpful insight into one book by comparing it with that author's other book or books.

5. And of course in its historical context, 1 John was written to a specific community with a specific situation in mind, namely, the departure of a group of Gnostics who had disassociated themselves from the church John was writing to.

6. Software and internet sources increasingly make it easy for any preacher to look up all the places in the Bible where a particular word is used.

HEAVEN OPENED

Unity of Scripture

Gareth Lee Cockerill

Then beginning with Moses and all the prophets, he interpreted to them the things about himself in all the scriptures.

—Luke 24:27 (NRSV)

Have a constant eye to the analogy of faith, the connection and harmony there is between those grand, fundamental doctrines, original sin, justification by faith, the new birth, inward and outward holiness.

—John Wesley, Preface to *Explanatory Notes Upon the Old Testament*

As the pastor announced his text I fumbled in my Bible to find the reference—Joel 2:28–32. "Let's see, where is Joel? Ezekiel, Daniel, Hosea, Joel . . . somewhere in here where the pages of my Bible are still stuck together. I guess I don't read these books very often," I mused with a silent laugh. My Bible is dog-eared in John. It falls open to the well-worn pages of Romans. But Joel?

As the pastor began the message, my mind went its own way pursuing its own questions. "Why does our Bible have these less-read books? Why is the pastor preaching from the Old Testament? Why does that seem unusual?" I began to think about the Bible in church history. Whatever else we may say, one thing is certain. All branches of the Christian church have always affirmed the importance and unity of the whole Bible. The earliest church fathers made a point of defending this unity vigorously against all heresies. Second-century leaders like Ignatius of Antioch, Irenaeus of Lyon, and Tertullian of Carthage were adamant that the Creator God of the Old Testament was the God and Father of our Lord Jesus Christ. The same God spoke through the same Holy Spirit to Moses, the prophets, and the New Testament apostles. Tertullian began the custom of referring to the one Scripture as the "Old" and "New" Testaments.

> Our Savior "is clearly defined to us in all Scriptures—in the Old Testament as the Christ of God, in the New Testament as the Son of God."
>
> —Tertullian, *Against Praxius*

Just then the preacher's voice broke through my reverie: "In Acts 2 Peter said that this prophecy was fulfilled on the day of Pentecost." Yes, the New Testament writers themselves believed the Old Testament was Scripture that had been fulfilled by Christ. The writer of Hebrews began his book, "At various times and in various ways the God who spoke of old to our Fathers has now spoken to us in one who is Son." When on trial for Christ, Paul declared, "And now I stand here on trial because of my hope in the promise made by God to our fathers" (Acts 26:6). Paul began Romans, his theological manifesto, by proclaiming that God had promised the gospel of his Son "beforehand through his prophets in the holy Scriptures" (Rom. 1:3).

These New Testament claims resonate with the expectations of Old Testament writers. God promised Abraham (Gen. 12) that through his descendants God would restore blessing to the rebellious nations of the world (Gen. 1–11). This promise was not fulfilled with either the settlement of the Promised Land under Joshua or the return from Exile following Cyrus's edict. The prophets looked forward to a fulfillment effected by the Messiah and characterized by

God's indwelling Spirit. If the New Testament is the key for understanding the Old, the key fits the lock. The pastor finished his sermon and I left the church with a deep appreciation for the harmony of the Bible.

PREACHING THE WHOLE BIBLE

The unity of Scripture becomes clear when we examine the nature of the Bible. Through the Bible God reveals himself to us in order to bring us into fellowship with himself as part of his redeemed people. Thus the whole Bible is the story of God's relationship with humanity. When we come to know him he invites us to identify with his people and make the biblical story our own. We begin to interpret our own life stories in light of the biblical drama of redemption.

Wedding anniversaries remind us that every interpersonal relationship has a history. If we forget an anniversary we belittle the relationship by ignoring its past. In like manner, if we neglect the whole story of Scripture we demean our relationship with God and have no basis for understanding its nature and significance.

Words can be confusing. "Story" makes some people think of fiction. On the other hand, "history" is often used to describe the historian's reconstruction of "what really happened." The Bible is the true revelation of God's relationship with humanity. We might call it a "historical story." Using various styles and many smaller stories, the Bible tells this one true story of God's bringing humanity into fellowship with himself. Within and through this story God reveals truth about himself, just as persons in ongoing relationships reveal truth about themselves to each other.

Bible preachers must remember two important things. First, our preaching should invite people to enter the biblical story and allow it to shape their individual stories. The Holy Spirit uses this biblical story to mold us into the image of Christ. Second, we must interpret each passage as part of the whole story. To interpret any passage as though it were disconnected from the whole of Scripture is misinterpretation.

Here are some practical guidelines that will help us invite people into the biblical story by preaching each text in light of the whole:

ACQUIRE "BIBLINE BLOOD"

We, as preachers, must live in that story ourselves. Nothing substitutes for the preacher's being saturated with the biblical story. John Wesley's very language was so permeated with Scripture that it is proper to call this man of wide reading a "man of one book." He had what some have described as "bibline blood." Deep familiarity with God's Word and with its Author is the foundation for all holistic interpretation and preaching.

> Humbly read [the books of] the Bible in order from beginning to end, so that you first get the simple story in your mind . . .
>
> —Martin Luther,
> *Letter to George Spalatin*

"Bibline blood" comes from reading and rereading the entire Bible through again and again. Sometimes it is good to read the Old and New Testaments simultaneously. I like to read the New in the morning and the Old in the evening. When we read several chapters at a time, thinking about what has gone before and what follows, we can better see what part these chapters play in the great story. Reading humbly and prayerfully is the means by which we pursue relationship with God. The Psalms are worthy of special attention. They record the inspired songs of praise and prayers of petition that provide a model and inspiration for our own devotion. Regular psalm reading is an important way of bathing our emotions and imagination in the story of God with his people.

KNOW THE STORY

We must study Scripture in its larger canonical divisions with attention to their differing characteristics, purposes, and relationships to one another. For instance, by introducing God, humanity, the world, and sin, Genesis 1–11 has a unique and foundational role in Scripture. God is the sovereign Creator who has a gracious purpose for His creation, is the sole Judge of its adequacy, and has blessed it.

God's creation is finite but meaningful, the place where God's blessing is to be enjoyed and His purposes are to be fulfilled. He made humanity in His image so human beings could: (1) have fellowship with Him; (2) live in harmonious fellowship as the people of God; and (3) responsibly enjoy the world He created. Eden is the happy place in which the first humans enjoyed the blessings of these three relationships. These chapters also show us that sin is distrust of God's goodness, disobedience of his command, and the attempt to displace God with self as the determiner of one's life (3:1–6). This foundational section of Scripture shows the power, corruption, and universality of sin and the ways it destroys all three of the God-intended blessed relationships.

God follows each judgment on disobedience described in Genesis 1–11 with a promise of redemption. This gracious promise crystallizes in God's covenant with Abraham (Genesis 12). God promised to bring Abraham's descendants into fellowship with himself, to make them a great nation in fellowship with one another, and to provide a new Eden, the blessed Promised Land. Thus, all three of the relationships lost in the original Eden would be restored.

But God's promise went even further. All nations of the earth, so recently turned away from God in Genesis 1–11, would be blessed. The vision of Abraham's children in the Promised Land is only a picture of God's ultimate restoration. Genesis 12–50 depicts the way this promise worked out in Abraham's family. We can identify with these people of God as they grew in faith, fell into temptation, were restored, reconciled, forgiven, and renewed. We see that God works even in dysfunctional families and relationships. We are invited to understand and to be encouraged in our own walk with God in light of theirs.

In the next five books of the Old Testament (Exodus through Joshua), God's promise moved from the family to the national level. He reestablished all three of the relationships lost in Eden. First, by delivering Abraham's descendants from Egypt he brought them into fellowship with himself, "I will be your God" (Ex. 6:7b). Second, by making covenant with them at Sinai he established them as a people, his people in fellowship with one another, "I will take you for My people" (Ex. 6:7a). The covenant showed them how to live in harmony. Finally, by giving them the Promised Land he provided for their enjoyment of creation. God's people could live in fellowship with Him, in harmony with one another, in a new Eden. No wonder Joshua could say, "You know with all your heart and soul that not one of all the good promises the Lord your God gave you has failed. Every promise has been fulfilled; not one has failed" (Josh. 23:14). Yet, as significant as this restoration through Moses and Joshua was, it did not reach to the far-flung nations of the world, nor, as Israel's disobedience would show, did it reach the depths of the human heart. God had more in store.

Judges through 2 Kings carries on the story of Israel's disobedience and God's continued judgment and mercy. Disobedience toward God always led to social disruption and to loss of the land's blessings. The picture at the end of Judges is far from people in fellowship with God, in harmony with one another, and enjoying the blessings of Canaan. God used Israel's request for a king and consequent rejection of His rule (1 Sam. 8) to choose David and his descendants as leaders who would "plant" Israel in obedience to God's covenant.

Along with David, He gave them the Temple as a visible embodiment of His presence and aid to their loyalty. The narrative of Kings, however, shows how both kings and people continued in the path of disobedience and degeneration that led to exile, the ultimate loss of the enjoyment of God's blessings. But the God who gave His promise to Abraham is faithful. Amid the story of this progressive degeneration, the prophets called for repentance and promised God's grace. As Israel persisted in disobedience, the prophets began to look for a new act of God, a new covenant of the Spirit, that would solve the problem of the willful and disobedient heart. The returned exiles remembered God's great blessings of the past with hope (Chronicles) because, although those blessings had not been restored (Ezra-Nehemiah), they believed God was still at work (Esther); thus they could trust His promises for the future.

> In what is said [by the Psalms] we hear of the one we call Lord. In the way it is said . . . we are given a model for our own response to God.
>
> —Patrick G. Miller

If the Old Testament looks forward to the reestablishment of what was lost in Eden and pictured in the Promised Land—a new humanity living in fellowship with God, in the harmony and wellbeing of covenantal wholeness, and in enjoyment of the environment provided by God—the New Testament proclaims that this hope has been fulfilled in Jesus Christ.

The Gospels narrate the wonderful fulfillment of this Old Testament hope and promise in the life, death, and resurrection of Jesus. While the first three, the "Synoptic" Gospels, relate this fundamental story from slightly different perspectives, John puts the icing on the cake through his deeper meditation upon that fulfillment. The blessed rule of God has been restored and eternal life is promised to those under the curse of death since the disobedience of Eden. Acts brings the story into the Christian present; this crucified and risen Jesus is present in His church through the Spirit. Here is a picture of the life of those who follow Him. If we had a shopping mall map of the Bible the sign would point to "Acts" and say "You are here."

> The apostles proclaimed one and the same God, . . . who gave [Abraham] the promise of inheritance, . . . who called his descendants out of Egypt . . . , [who was] the Maker of all things, . . . the Father of our Lord Jesus Christ, . . . the God of glory.
>
> —Irenaeus, *Against Heresies*

The New Testament letters proclaim the heartbeat of the apostles and teachers of the early church, a message addressed to people who live in the spiritual age depicted in Acts. Finally, the Revelation focuses on the grand climax of the story, on the return of the Lord and the undying reality of life with Him in the eternal Zion and Promised Land.

These few paragraphs paint in very broad strokes some of the groupings of and relationships between the biblical books, essential to grasping the whole story.

LISTEN FOR THE CLUES PROVIDED BY THE BIBLICAL WRITERS

The Biblical writers were conscious of being part of this grand story. Thus they show us in their writings how each part fits into the larger scheme. If we will listen for the clues they have given us, we will be able to see how their individual writings contribute to the whole.

Take one New Testament story for example: Jesus entered the Temple at the beginning of Holy Week and asserted His authority over it by driving out the sellers of merchandise. The parable of the Wicked Tenants in Mark 12:1–12 is His answer to the rulers when they asked what right He had to do such a thing. The opening verses strike an Isaianic chord. Jesus' description of the vineyard certainly reminded His hearers of Isaiah's "Song of the Vineyard" (Isa. 5:1–5). In this metaphorical love song, God is the gracious Husbandman who has done all for His vineyard while Judah is the faithless vineyard (lover) with no gratitude for God's goodness. Thus we immediately know Jesus was telling a story involving the history of God's goodness and His people's ingratitude.

As the story unfolds, we see that the owner was God, the tenants were the Judean rulers, the servants were God's prophets sent throughout Old Testament times. Jesus, as the "owner's" Son, is both greatly superior to the prophets and the fulfillment of all their prophetic oracles. If the Temple leadership rejected Him, as they were about to do, they would be rejecting the whole history of God's gracious self-revelation and provision.

This story reaches its resolution in the stone-being-rejected passage Jesus quoted from Psalm 118:22–23. To reject Jesus by not giving the fruit of faithfulness is to spurn God's whole story of redemption. Such disregard for God is the height of gross ingratitude and an act with the direst consequences. Those who reject Jesus are separated from God's people and God's blessing. However, the God who works in unexpected ways would take their very rejection of Jesus and make it the fulfillment of salvation's story.

Sometimes the clues offered by the biblical author for understanding a passage in light of the whole are not as obvious as in the above passage, but they are often far more obvious than we realize. For instance, John 1:14 affirms that the Son's becoming a human being is analogous to and the fulfillment of God's dwelling with His people in the Old Testament Tabernacle. John then explains Jesus' cleansing of the Temple in chapter two as Jesus' declaration that His body is now the true Temple, that in Him the God who once inhabited the Most Holy Place of Tabernacle and Temple now dwells among human beings (John 2:13–22).

In John 1:50, Jesus declared that the whole book of John would be a "Bethel" experience in which the reader, if he or she will, can see "the heaven opened" and God descending. When Jesus changed the water into wine at the wedding feast, He affirmed that what He brings fulfills, overflows, and ultimately displaces by abundant completion everything anticipated by the Israelite rites of purification (cf. John 2:6). We never will feel the force of the cross for Paul unless we understand the significance of Deuteronomy's imprecation, "Cursed is everyone who hangs upon a tree" (Gal. 3:13; Deut. 21:23).

Too often we pay great attention to the details of a text, but lose sight of these essential connections with the larger whole. We may discuss the etymology of words but lose track of their meaning within the passage and the greater story of God's revelation. We may strain at grammatical forms and forget that only their larger connections give them significance.

The more we are familiar with the whole story the more readily we will discern the clues within a passage that locate it within that whole. References to biblical persons and characteristic biblical expressions often are important. Thus, more "literal" translations, such as the New American Standard Bible and the English Standard Version, are often most helpful in seeing these connections. They tend, where possible and appropriate, to translate a Greek or Hebrew word by the same English expression so that word associations readily apparent to the first readers are apparent to us as well. They maintain the great words like "repentance," "faith," "righteousness," "sanctification," and "redemption," so we can see how Scripture develops these themes. The clues to understanding a passage in the light of the whole are often also the welcome mats that invite us and our hearers into this great story of God's love.

OUR HERITAGE AND OUR BLESSING

It is evident that there are no shortcuts to holistic biblical preaching. Biblical preachers will nurture "bibline blood" through constantly reading and re-reading the whole Bible. They will note the larger sections of Scripture and observe what each contributes to the whole. Finally, they will look for the clues which show how each passage is related to the whole. Real biblical preaching is the result of a lifestyle of biblical immersion and a lifetime of careful listening to God's voice in the text. If you do these things, "you will save yourself and your hearers" (1 Tim. 4:13).

John Wesley certainly was a man of the richest "bibline blood"; his whole life and ministry were saturated in the scriptural story. The normal language of his sermons reflects the biblical turn of phrase. He was thoroughly familiar with the central truths of Scripture, of God's story, and he kept them central. Thus he urged Bible readers to attend the grand themes of Scripture that give it unity, such truths as "original sin, justification by faith, the new birth, inward and outward holiness." The end of this story was indeed, "the way to heaven."

Someone has said Wesley made the "main thing the main thing," but many of his followers have "made the main thing the only thing." I have tried to help us correct this weakness by pointing out that the Bible is the story of God's revealing himself so as to bring people into fellowship with himself as part of the redeemed people of God. Remembering this truth keeps us from focusing too narrowly on our own "experience." Yes, we are transformed, but only through our coming into fellowship with God as part of His renewed people who are also in fellowship with Him. The ultimate goal of this fellowship is a renewed humanity living in communion with a Holy God. Thus, redemption is within the context of the church, of ethics, of last things, and, of course, of God himself.

Indeed, when we keep redemption rooted in this larger context we do exactly what the early church Fathers did. They argued that the "Rule of Faith" was the main theme, the uniting theme, of Scripture. By the rule of faith, the Fathers affirmed their belief in God as Creator of the world and Father of our Lord Jesus Christ. They affirmed the reality of the incarnation, death, resurrection, and ascension of Christ. They signified their belief in the present activity of the Holy Spirit applying the work of Christ in forgiveness and renewal, the second coming of Christ in glory, and eternal life in God's kingdom for the faithful. Thus they proclaimed the great truths of redemption within this larger framework of God's provision for a renewed humanity in fellowship with Him.

> One of our fundamental pastoral tasks is to teach our congregations to find themselves in the stories of Israel and the early church. . . . Rather than seeking to make the text relevant, Paul seeks to draw his readers *into* the text in such a way that its world reshapes the norms and decisions of the community in the present.
>
> —Richard B. Hays

It is, therefore, our charge to preach from each passage of Scripture so as to invite our hearers into the story of God's redemptive ways with humanity. When we preach thus, we are faithful to Scripture and to the heritage the Church has bequeathed to us. When we preach thus, the gospel can become eternally profitable for ourselves and for our hearers. Both they and we can take our places in the story of the faithful, described in Hebrews 11:1—12:29 as stretching from Abel to the Judgment. The Bible will become what John Wesley declared it to be, the Book that shows "the way to heaven."

ACTION SUGGESTIONS

1. Begin in Matthew and read one to two chapters of the New Testament each morning. Begin in Genesis and read two to three chapters from the Old Testament every evening. Consistent pursuit of this plan will take you through the Bible within two years. Use a different version each time you read the Bible through.

2. Choose a section of the Canon and begin to read and study it as a whole. You might begin with Genesis 1–11 or Genesis 12–50. You might select Exodus through Joshua, focusing on the narrative portions.

3. When you study a passage, begin to look for clues that show how it relates to other parts of Scripture. Note, for example, persons named in more than one place, terms used in multiple passages, and other biblical passages cited or referred to. Use the cross-references in your Bible. Ask yourself why the writer referred to these other scriptures.

FOR FURTHER READING

Achtemeier, Elizabeth. *Preaching from the Old Testament.* Louisville: Westminster/John Knox Press, 1985.

This is a clear and practical guide to preaching from the Old Testament, by one who loved Scripture and mastered sermon-craft. One need not agree with Achtemeier's critical assumptions to benefit from her work.

Oswalt, John N. *Called to Be Holy: A Biblical Perspective.* Nappanee: Evangel Publishing House, 1999.

A model of how to understand each part of the Bible in light of the whole, Oswalt's study is a must for biblical preaching on the holy life.

Wright, Christopher J. H. *Knowing Jesus through the Old Testament.* Downers Grove: InterVarsity Press, 1992.

Wright shows how the Bible presents Christ as the fulfillment of the Old Testament. A serious reading of this book will enrich preaching from both "halves" of the Bible.

Wright, Christopher J. H. *Old Testament Ethics for the People of God*. Downers Grove: InterVarsity Press, 2004.

A stimulating and thought-provoking work on the ethical role of the Old Testament for Christians, especially helpful in an age of moral confusion.

I LOVE TO TELL THE STORY

Preaching Basics

R. Duane Thompson and R. Duane Thompson II

All Jesus did that day was tell stories—a long storytelling afternoon. His storytelling fulfilled the prophecy: I will open my mouth and tell stories; I will bring out into the open Things hidden since the world's first day.

—Matthew 13:34–35 *(The Message)*

My dear sister, I am glad to hear that you found benefit by your little journey to Bristol. I did not doubt, but the conversation of those experienced Christians would be of service to you; and would enable you to be of more service to the little flock at Cheltenham. . . . From time to time, you should tell me just what God works in you, and by you.

—John Wesley, letter to Miss Newman, October 23, 1772

The prophet Nathan knew something about King David, something sordid. Nathan didn't waste any time wondering whether he was going to challenge the king or simply keep this information to himself—he, like all the Old Testament prophets, was in the business of confronting wrong. Still, this must have created a dilemma for Nathan. He had to determine precisely how he was going get David to see things God's way. It wouldn't help simply to name the sin—David had evidently grown quite comfortable with the seduction of Bathsheba and the murder of Uriah the Hittite; Nathan needed to convince the king of the offense of the crime. Nathan marched into the throne room and told a story, enticing David into a fictional world where David could actually experience the horror and sordidness of these deeds of his. "Show, don't tell" is how a writer or public speaker today might express it. Nathan helped David catch a glimpse of himself in a new and compelling way.

Nathan's story was not overly religious or sacred. It was just a natural, ordinary, very human story of a rich man with many sheep and cattle who stole a poor man's lone ewe lamb that was like a daughter to him. It intrigued the listener enough so that by the time Nathan was finished with his story David "burned with anger" (NIV). He claimed that because the rich man did all this with no pity he "deserved to die."

Nathan pointed directly at David and said, "You are the man."

The matter was settled, the case closed, no more evidence needed to be presented because the instance of recognition had occurred. David could no longer fool himself. He knew that the man without pity deserved to die, and he recognized that he himself was that man (2 Sam. 12).

Today we would scarcely know how to handle the prophets who pestered the kings and people of Israel. What would you do with that type of person? Invite him to a dinner party (one can almost see John the Baptist coming to such a banquet looking for locusts and wild honey)? Offer him the front-row pew on a Sunday morning? These were men who could look right through you with the eyes of God and were all too willing to tell you what they saw—good or bad. No, we wouldn't know now, as they didn't know then, just what to do with the prophets.

And yet, you, as preacher, are called to be that kind of person. You have a purpose, a message, an audience, and a method—just as every good prophet did.

PURPOSE

The goal of preaching is not to get the message only into your own head and heart; it is to get it into the hearts of the hearers, into their beings, into their lives. As Henry Ward Beecher wrote long ago, "It is not enough that men shall *know*. They must *be*."[1]

Perhaps many can be convinced intellectually of the truth of atonement, for instance. But the goal is not only to have people be convinced intellectually of any theological lesson. That may be the teacher's task, the teacher in seminary, and even the teacher in Sunday school or adult Bible study; but it should not be the main task or motivation of the preacher. The preacher's task is to have the people

> It is not enough that men shall *know*. They must *be*.
>
> —Henry Ward Beecher

in the pews *experience* the truth. As regards atonement: they must experience their own sin, the guilt and remorse over what they have done, the sense of hopelessness of ever getting themselves out of what they have gotten themselves into. They must ultimately experience Jesus coming into their lives to pay the price and get them out of their own evil predicament. The objective is not to have people quote Bible passages that talk about what atonement is; the objective is to build their character on the basis of the atonement, to help them build a life on the foundation of what God has done for them.

MESSAGE

YOU HAVE SINNED

Just as Nathan had to say to David, "You are the guilty one," so one of the tasks of the preacher is to tell John and Jane Doe they deserve to die (and then to help them know how they can live). It may not seem this is what they deserve at the time as they sit in the congregation in their Sunday finest, on their best behavior, with Mom's roast beef and mashed potatoes waiting for them when they get home. But that is precisely the point: life and death—even in church, even when it is the stated topic of conversation—seem awfully abstract and theoretical most of the time. It is not easy to get the message through to people.

> Narrative . . . is the way that truth comes to me—not in crisp propositions but in messy tales of encounters between people and people, between people and creation, between people and God.
>
> —Barbara Brown Taylor, "Never-ending Story"

Fifty-year members need to be reminded of sin, too, because they sometimes forget. Certainly, they know sin is in the world, and they see sin in other people; but they forget they themselves are prone to sin and need God's grace daily themselves. They may feel archly superior to those still gripped in the devastating clutches of a sinful life, which reveals only that they are gripped by one of the deadliest sins of all: pride.

YOU ARE FORGIVEN

Telling people of their sin, of course, is only the beginning. The heart of the Wesleyan message is forgiveness, both giving it and receiving it. For Wesley the reality of the story of the Second Person of the Trinity becoming human was the foundation of forgiveness and salvation. Wesleyans believe that God has sacrificed his Son that we might receive forgiveness for our sins. This places a significant obligation on us to grant forgiveness to others who have offended us.

Of course, the point of speaking to people about forgiveness is not to have them simply define it or to quote scripture verses on it. Many people go home from church knowing all about forgiveness without ever practicing it, not even really giving it much of a try. In other words, they haven't experienced it. Oh, sure, they believe it in some abstract sense that doesn't seem to apply to them; but if they knew what it was to receive the grace of God, they would no longer wonder if forgiveness really works. They would believe it at a deep level and use it in their daily lives as a way to resolve the problems they encounter.

AUDIENCE

Preachers may be speaking to those who would just as soon not listen to what they have to say. Concepts that energize us preachers may bore our listeners. People come to church for all kinds of reasons, many of which have absolutely nothing to do with our preaching. Of course, it's the highlight for us, because we are doing it, but the sermon often is the point in the service when a portion of the congregation tunes out slightly, even turns off completely. We must face the fact that not everyone present is waiting expectantly for our next word. A wise, old preacher once said, "You have to remember that half your congregation almost didn't come to church today." Moreover, the other half likely has pressing burdens and problems that make any message irrelevant this day.

Now this may not be your congregation. The old preacher's statement may be a bit of an exaggeration with regard to any congregation. But it's certainly true that people will eventually stop attending church (or go elsewhere) if they are not being fed, if they are not getting what they need. The basic reason people come to your service, whether they realize it or not, is to meet some need, to be filled, to find the place of rest for their restless hearts, as Augustine put it. Your job is to give expression to the need, to ask aloud the questions in their hearts and minds, then to propose the solutions only God can provide.

METHOD

BE ENGAGING

Some theological concepts are difficult to explain; but putting these ideas in the form of a tangible, compelling story or image will get people to own the concepts themselves. ("We laughed; we cried.") The key is to engage them. You may have memories of old-time camp meetings and revivals in which the preacher would ask the congregation near the end of the sermon to consider what would happen if they left the tabernacle or the church that evening and were hit by a bus or had a heart attack. Where would they spend eternity? Suddenly, in the emotional fever pitch of the closing moments of such a service, perhaps with *Just As I Am* playing softly in the background, immortality and eternity, life and death, heaven and the other place, can seem awfully close at hand.

FIND A COMMON LANGUAGE

You may find that even the most inattentive become the most authentic hearers of the Word once the deepest questions and answers of their souls—the questions and answers of the Bible and the Christian faith—are addressed in ways they understand. Don't speak in Bible-ese or abstract theological concepts but in a language and a manner people can understand.

The objective is not only to speak but to be heard—to find the place and the language where a connection is made.

Charles Colson confronted this issue with an acquaintance who was intrigued by Colson's Christian commitment, but who didn't believe in and didn't want to hear anything about Jesus Christ. Colson tried to jumpstart the conversation by talking about what will happen when we die, but he was cut off by the man's statement that death was merely the end; he did not believe in an afterlife. Any mention of the Bible then, by Colson, had a predictable outcome, confirmed when this man put his hand up, palm outward, and claimed firmly, "All legends."

"What could I say?" Colson writes. "He didn't care about God's plan for his life, getting into heaven, or what the Bible said." Colson wondered if he would ever have any way to discuss his faith with this man. Then an idea popped into his head. He asked the man if he'd seen Woody Allen's movie *Crimes and Misdemeanors*. This led into a discussion of conscience and how we deal with ourselves when we do something wrong. These issues had given the man a great deal of concern. Colson next brought up Tolstoy's *War and Peace* and then some of the writings of C. S. Lewis. The man was familiar with these and willing to engage in conversation about them. These conversations led, in turn, to deeper things.

> Without Woody Allen, Leo Tolstoy, and C. S. Lewis, I wouldn't have found a common ground and language with which to discuss the spiritual realm with [my friend].
>
> —Charles Colson,
> *Being the Body*

Colson wrote that he wasn't sure what would happen with his friend. He hadn't turned his life over to Christ as of the writing of Colson's book. "But," he reported, "I know one thing: Without Woody Allen, Leo Tolstoy, and C. S. Lewis, I wouldn't have found a common ground and language with which to discuss the spiritual realm with him."[2]

Common language to create a common ground is the hallmark of good communication.

GO THROUGH THE BACK DOOR

Good communication is at work also in the writings of J. R. R. Tolkien and the recent movies based on his *Lord of the Rings* trilogy. "Tolkien's myth and fantasy can open the heart's back door when the front door is locked," two writers have claimed with regard to both the books and the movies. "The result has been that millions, many of whom reject formal religion, have encountered realities that flourish in the unexpected regions of Christian belief."[3]

STORYTELLING

The Bible is a book of stories. Some books are nothing but stories; others use stories and illustrations of various sorts. Even the life of Jesus—the way He approached people, the way He responded to them, laid His hands on them, healed them, and sometimes rebuked them and was angered by them—is a story that fleshes out our concept of God. Not only does the Bible contain stories, it is a story. The theme of this sixty-six-book story is salvation. The plot, full of suspense and surprise, varies; it thickens, concludes, and metamorphoses into new plots. Storytellers down through the ages have looked to the Bible as a model of what a story should be. As Elie Wiesel said, "God made man because he loves stories."[4]

> Tolkien's myth and fantasy can open the heart's back door when the front door is locked.
>
> —Kurt Bruner and Jim Ware,
> *Finding God in the
> Lord of the Rings*

Some of the things God wants to tell His people can be conveyed only through story. For instance, stories can create a scene that shows how difficult forgiveness is and another to reveal how the impossible can be made possible. Take the story of the seminary student who wanted desperately for God to use him in a mighty way: One summer day, as he drove a city bus to earn tuition money, three young toughs boarded. They refused to pay then began to hassle other passengers. The seminary student flagged down a police officer who forced the rabble-rousers to pay the fare. When the policeman left the bus, the three passengers beat up the seminary student. While his wounds healed, he thought of all he had given up and considered dropping out of seminary.

The three young men were caught and convicted. At the sentencing, the seminary student saw his attackers again, no longer tough and swaggering hotshots but instead frightened and remorseful young men. He stood up, asked permission to address the court, and offered to serve their sentences for them. The judge did not permit this; but for the first time in their lives these young men realized someone cared about them. Later, after the seminary student visited them in prison, they came to understand that God loved them. This, the seminary student realized, was the great work God had called him to that summer.[5]

A similar story is told of a chicken thief within a Native American tribe: The chief declared that, if caught, the offender would receive ten lashes. When the thefts didn't stop, the number of lashes was raised to twenty, then fifty, and finally to one hundred, a sure death sentence. Of course, the thief was caught eventually—the chief's own mother.

Everyone wondered if the chief's love for his mother would override his sense of justice; but when the time came, his mother was tied to the whipping post. However, instead of using the whip himself, he handed it to a strong, young man at his side. Then he wrapped his arms around his mother in a protective embrace and ordered the warrior to give *him* the hundred lashes.[6]

Stories also create the atmosphere in which truth, old or new, can break through the defenses we all put up to guard ourselves from the painful encounter with our own sin. Those defenses must be broken down for the message to get through.

Stories engage the reader. Barbara Brown Taylor writes that she is "one of those listeners who consistently remembers the stories and forgets the points. That is because the points tend to be perfectly clear and well behaved, as very little in [her] life ever is, while the stories (at least the good ones) star flawed characters with muddy motives whom [she] recognizes at once." When she herself preaches, then, she continues, "Narrative is not a choice I make when it comes time to tell the truth; it is the way that truth comes to me—not in crisp propositions but in messy tales of encounters between people and people, between people and creation, between people and God."[7]

Think of this favorite old story, for instance: Two rich brothers were well known in their small town for being swindlers in their business dealings. One brother died; the other came to the minister to discuss the funeral service. Fearing what could be told of the deceased, he made the minister an offer. "If you call my brother a saint during the eulogy, you have my word that this little wad of cash will be yours." He held up the money for the minister to see. After a moment of consideration the minister agreed.

When the funeral hour arrived, the church was packed. Many in attendance had been swindled by the two brothers through the years. They knew nothing of the deal between the minister and the surviving brother, but were anxious to hear how the minister would handle the situation. Finally, the moment arrived, and the minister stood to give the eulogy. "The man you see before you in this coffin was a vile and debauched individual," he began. "He was a manipulator, a deceiver, a liar, and a reprobate. He destroyed the fortunes, careers and lives of countless people in this town, many of whom are here today. This man did every evil, rotten, and unconscionable thing you can imagine. But, compared to his brother, who's sitting right over there, the man in this coffin was a saint."

Ravi Zacharias writes that he loves to use this story because it captures something universal: the shortcomings of each human being. He reports telling it at a conference with delegates from all over the world. In watching the videotape later, he could see that every face lit up with uproarious laughter and recognition.[8]

The wonderful thing about the best stories is that they can have several different meanings. You may use a story to make one point, but the minds of many in the congregation may race ahead, faster than you can speak, to uses and applications in other areas of their lives. In this way you may do more good than you know. You may or may not make the point you intended, but in telling a story you may still leave your congregation something inspiring, useful, and good—something you hadn't even thought of.

> God made man because he loves stories.
>
> —Elie Wiesel

Stories are the "stuff" of life. The Bible contains stories of real people. The Bible and people of all periods of history have much in common that can be communicated by intermingling biblical and other historical and contemporary stories. To fail to use any of these resources is to shrink one's basis for a flourishing ministry. The use of all these resources will provide freshness to minister and congregation alike.

In *The Arabian Nights* the king married a succession of virgins, each of whom was executed after his first night with her. But Scheherazade, the king's latest bride, wisely told the king stories, saying, "What is this compared with what I shall tell you tomorrow night if the king spares me and lets me live?" So her life was spared night after night to complete the story. If you as a pastor learn to tell a good story, you may save a person from spiritual death. You may also breathe new life into your own ministry and enjoy life extension.

ACTION SUGGESTIONS

1. Use some of your reading and study time to read novels, short stories (those of O. Henry, for example), history, biographies, and autobiographies. Not only will you find stories, illustrations, and quotes; this will help you develop a more narrative way of expressing yourself.

2. Read books composed exclusively of stories and illustrations; a good example is *The Tale of the Tardy Oxcart and 1,501 Other Stories*, by Charles Swindoll. Read human interest stories in magazines and newspapers.

3. Read the cartoons ("funny pages") in the newspaper. Anthologies of *Peanuts* and *Calvin and Hobbes* are especially rich sources.

4. Little stories happen around us all the time. Be on the lookout for the way people (including *yourself*) interact with other people and react to unusual or unforeseen circumstances and situations.

FOR FURTHER READING

Campolo, Tony. *Let Me Tell You a Story*. Nashville: Word Publishing Co., 2001.

This is a rich collection of stories that speak plainly to a variety of life situations and theological issues.

Craddock, Fred B. *Overhearing the Gospel*. St. Louis: Chalice Press, 2002.

Craddock attempts to answer the question, "How does one person communicate the Christian faith to another?" by emphasizing the critical value of indirect communication. This provides the basis for understanding his unusual style of preaching.

Graves Mike, and **Ward**, R. F., eds. *Craddock Stories*. St. Louis: Chalice Press, 2001.

The stories of Fred Craddock are creative and unique. Sometimes wry and humorous, sometimes serious, almost dark, Craddock has a way of penetrating straight to the listener's heart—and to the heart of the theological matter.

Swindoll, Charles. *The Tale of the Tardy Oxcart, and 1,501 Other Stories*. Nashville: Word Publishing Co., 1998.

This is the single best source for popular poems, illustrations and stories, both humorous and serious, and almost always thought-provoking.

NOTES

1. Lyman Abbott, *Henry Ward Beecher* (Cambridge, MA: Piligrim Press, 1903), 355.

2. Charles Colson and Ellen Vaughn, *Being the Body* (Nashville: W Publishing Group, 2003), 371–372.

3. Kurt Bruner and Jim Ware, *Finding God in the Lord of the Rings* (Wheaton, IL: Tyndale, 2001), x.

4. Charles E. Winquist, "Homecoming: Interpretation, Transformation, and Individuation," *AAR Studies in Religion* 18 (1978), 2.

5. Charles R Swindoll, *The Tale of the Tardy Oxcart*, and 1,501 Other Stories (Nashville: Word, 1998), 542–543.

6. Dennis Fisher, "Does God Grade on a Curve?" *Discovery Series* (Grand Rapids: RBC Ministries, 2003), 18.

7. Barbara Brown Taylor, "Never-ending Story," *Christian Century* (March 8, 2003), 37.

8. Ravi Zacharias, *Can Man Live Without God* (Dallas: Word, 1994), 135–136.

GOOD NEWS FOR A HURTING WORLD

Social Justice

Paul Shea

> *The Spirit of the Lord is upon me, because he has anointed me to preach good news to the poor. He has sent me to proclaim freedom for the prisoners and recovery of sight for the blind, to release the oppressed, to proclaim the year of our Lord's favor.*
>
> —Luke 4:18–19, Quoting Isaiah 61:1–2b

> *The Christian does good unto all men; unto neighbor and strangers, friends and enemies, and at that in every possible kind, not only to their bodies by feeding the hungry, clothing the naked, visiting those that are sick or in prison, but much more does he labor to do good to their souls.*
>
> —John Wesley, *The Character of a Methodist*

I t was the twenty-fifth annual observance of Earth Day. During a regular chapel service—after reading psalms on the glories of creation, singing songs such as "How Great Thou Art," presenting original poetry on nature, and giving an exhortation on the stewardship of the earth—the speaker asked the audience of about one thousand evangelical and Wesleyan college students how many had heard a sermon on the environment in the last year. About four hands went up. Perhaps Wesleyan folk are just squeamish about environmental issues. The percentage likely would have been higher for other social concerns such as poverty, materialism, AIDS, fair trade, genocide, bioethics, euthanasia, abortion, human trafficking, displaced peoples, unemployment, or international violence.

How frequently should pastors preach on subjects of social justice? Does the Bible even advocate meddling in such worldly topics? Isn't the job of the preacher to convince sinners to repent, to offer the amazing gift of salvation in Christ, and to nurture believers for spiritual growth and outreach? Is it wise to preach on subjects that stir up controversy and detract from the main task of lifting up Christ?

During my pilgrimage of Christian service, two sources have provided significant guidance through these minefields. The first is our theological roots, the stirring model of John Wesley in his day of social unrest. The second is the broad biblical witness to the themes of justice and God's holistic purposes, the focal point being the convincing example of the Master Preacher himself, Jesus.

WESLEYAN ROOTS

My journey to advocating prayerful, thoughtful, and biblical preaching on social issues began in a Wesleyan preacher's home where compassion for the poor and marginalized was nobly demonstrated. Eloquent preaching is no substitute for genuine Spirit-filled acts of mercy. It was godly actions coinciding with true words that convinced me Christ is real. Later God led me to one of the least developed countries of the world, Sierra Leone, West Africa, where in the midst of poverty, illness, and spiritual power struggles the gospel—in word and deed—was alive. Spiritual, social, and physical concerns were addressed together. Hospitals, schools, and development projects, along with many hardly-noticed deeds of mercy and kindness, delivered the message of the church.

To understand how I arrived in Sierra Leone and at this comprehensive view of the Bible's concern for issues of justice and mercy, we must rewind to earlier in my story—and to our Wesleyan roots.

Concern for social justice gradually became a top priority for me. While my high school buddies fought in Vietnam, and university campuses were awash in protest, my Christian college days included demonstrations on sideburns and hair length. After college, at the urging of an uncle who thought I needed to experience urban issues, I attended seminary near Chicago where the heat of war protests, political dissent, and racial tensions

> The Christian does good unto all men; unto neighbor and strangers, friends and enemies, and at that in every possible kind, not only to their bodies by feeding the hungry, clothing the naked, visiting those that are sick or in prison, but much more does he labor to do good to their souls.
>
> —John Wesley, *The Character of a Methodist*

were amplified. My fellow seminarians engaged in debates and activism; my African-American friends and professors leveled their critique of the white church; and my experience of human needs broadened in that urban context.

Shaken by this new awakening to contemporary realities and uncertainties, I renewed a search for confirmation of my denominational heritage—and I was astonished to discover the social intensity at the roots of British and American Wesleyanism.

What was John Wesley's social message to eighteenth-century England? Some historians have credited the evangelical preachers with saving England from the upheaval that swept France. Wesley was a traveling preacher, a churchman—not a politician—but he addressed nearly every social issue: politics, war, education, money, poverty, liquor, treatment of prisoners, and, of course, slavery.

What struck me as I dug into Wesley's sermons was the clear two-fold nature of his social message. I expected, and found, Wesley's powerful preaching of personal salvation that resulted in conversion and radical change in thousands of common folks. Every day Wesley preached to throngs, met with new believers, and shepherded his leaders.

> Where is the justice of inflicting the severest evils on those who have done us no wrong? Of depriving those that never injured us in word or deed, of every comfort of life?
>
> —John Wesley,
> *Thoughts on Slavery*

These regenerated and sanctified believers then became the catalyst for profound social change. According to Wesley, the new Christian "does good unto all men; unto neighbor and strangers, friends and enemies, and at that in every possible kind, not only to their bodies by feeding the hungry, clothing the naked, visiting those that are sick or in prison, but much more does he labor to do good to their souls."[1] Wesley practiced what he preached by giving to the poor, feeding the hungry, and helping the orphans and uneducated. He not only preached about the works that follow salvation, but he published numerous pamphlets and articles on the fruits of Christian perfection in everyday life.[2]

The social ill of slavery drew his special attention and highlighted the second element in Wesley's message. Here he moved from reliance on changed hearts to advocacy for political or radical social change. In 1774 his concern born out of broad reading resulted in his own published pamphlet, *Thoughts on Slavery,* with its appeal to natural human justice and morality:

This is the plain, unaggravated matter of fact. Such is the manner wherein our African slaves are procured; such the manner wherein they are removed from their native land, and wherein they are treated in our plantations. I would not inquire whether they can be defended, on the principles of even heathen honesty; whether they can be reconciled (setting the Bible out of the question) with any degree of either justice or mercy. . . . Where is the justice of inflicting the severest evils on those who have done us no wrong? Of depriving those that never injured us in word or deed, of every comfort of life?[3]

Wesley pled for an end to slavery with the nation, with slave traders, with all who would listen. By 1787 the Committee for the Abolition of Slave Trade was formed by his friend Thomas Clarkson and others. Wesley quickly endorsed them, saying it was "a truly Christian design, to procure, if possible, an Act of Parliament for the abolition of slavery. . . . Mr. Clarkson's design strikes at the root of it."[4] He added:

What little I can do to promote this excellent work I shall do with pleasure. I will print a large edition of the tract I wrote some years since, *Thoughts on Slavery,* and send it to all my friends in Great Britain and Ireland; adding a few words in favor of your design.[5]

Four years later, February 26, 1791, Wesley's last known correspondence was to parliamentarian William Wilberforce who was fighting for the cause of abolition. Wesley wrote, "If God be for you, who can be against you? . . . Go on, in the name of God and in the

> The God of the biblical revelation, being both Creator and Redeemer, is a God who cares about the total well-being (spiritual and material) of all the human beings he has made.
>
> —John R. W. Stott, *The Contemporary Christian*

power of his might, till even American slavery (the vilest that ever saw the sun) shall vanish away before it."[6]

Wesley, this greatest of all our preachers, lived, breathed, acted, and preached for justice and social change while also preaching salvation of souls and profound change in individual lives through the power of the Spirit. Others like Orange Scott in New England forty years later followed in his footsteps at a cost. By 1844 the scripturally inspired abolitionist preaching and protesting of Scott and his friends resulted in expulsion from the Methodist Episcopal Church and the formation of the Wesleyan Methodist Connection.

BIBLICAL GROUNDS FOR SOCIAL JUSTICE

Did our theological forebears have grounds for leaping into the world of human rights, human hurts, justice, or politics in our busy lives and in our preaching? Do we? One of the world's most admired evangelicals, British pastor, global teacher and theologian, Dr. John R. W. Stott, observes:

The God of the biblical revelation, being both Creator and Redeemer, is a God who cares about the total well-being (spiritual and material) of all the human beings he has made. . . . He begs them to listen to his word, to return to him in penitence, and to receive his forgiveness. On the other hand, God cares for the poor and the hungry, the alien, the widow and the orphan. He denounces oppression and tyranny, and calls for justice. He tells his people to be the voice of the voiceless and the defender of the powerless, and so to express their love for them. It is neither an accident nor a surprise, therefore, that God's two great commandments are that we love him with all our being and our neighbors as ourselves.[7]

The biblical case for holistic preaching centers in the Creation and the Fall in the Old Testament and in Jesus in the New Testament.

CREATION, FALL, PREPARATION FOR RESTORATION

The first three chapters of Genesis are vital to all preaching and theology. God created the world and everything in it and "it was good." God's Lord*ship* was in place when the relation*ship* between God and people was open, His owner*ship* of the earth was recognized, and human steward*ship* of the earth was accepted (Gen. 1:26–30). Wholeness in the world order of things is manifested under God's Lordship.[8]

Immediately after sin entered the picture (Gen. 3) physical, social, and spiritual chaos broke loose. The relationship between God and humans was broken, stewardship of the earth was neglected, and the earth fell out of sorts. The rest of the Bible tells the story of God's work to restore the wholeness that once existed. Reconciliation of people to God and to each other is necessary and is fulfilled in the Cross of Christ (Eph. 1:7; 2:13; Col. 1:21–22). Even the physical world of creation joins in awaiting a final restoration (Rom. 8:22).

> God's love for justice is grounded in God's love for each and every one of God's human creatures.
>
> —Nicholas Wolterstorff, "The God Who Loves Justice . . ."

When we see our world in a mess and needing repair, we know why. We preachers of the Bible story should know, too, how it is fixed on all levels, for that is the redemption story of the Bible.

Of course, we know God selected God's people Israel to work on his rescue and restoration project. Through a long, drawn-out, painful process, God shed light on how his people should behave toward one another and toward the hurting world. God gave instruction about helping the stranger, the widow, the poor, and those in debt. This includes, for example, instruction on redemption, the Sabbath year, the year of Jubilee, the tithe, interest on loans, and gleaning (Lev. 25; Deut. 14:22–29; 15:1–11; 23:19–20; 24:19–22).

These and many other Pentateuchal texts make clear that God has a special place in His heart for the poor and helpless. Psalm 103:6 is a good summary: "The Lord works righteousness and justice for all the oppressed." This theme reverberates throughout the Old Testament. Often it was in the hearts and on the lips of God's preachers, the prophet/poets of Israel. Amos was the first, "For three sins of Israel, even for four, I will not turn back my wrath. They sell the righteous for silver, and the needy for a pair of sandals. They trample on the heads of the poor and upon the dust of the ground and deny justice to the oppressed" (Amos 2:6–7). Isaiah spoke as eloquently, "Stop doing wrong, learn to do right! Seek justice, encourage the oppressed. Defend the cause of the fatherless, plead the case of the widow" (Isa. 1:17).

> Justice consists of enjoying those goods, those components of one's shalom, to which one is morally entitled. So of course God loves justice and hates injustice.
>
> —Nicholas Wolterstorff, "The God Who Loves Justice . . ."

A favorite description of God's intention for all people is the rich word *shalom*—meaning wholeness, harmony, peace in every area and aspect of life, individually and communally. The concept of *shalom* offers many glimpses of God's present and future purpose for whole and blessed living. If you ever wondered whether God cared for tangible things like infant mortality, housing, the elderly, prosperous gardens—in short, for whole, peaceful, and abundant living—you only have to search the Old Testament for occurrences of *shalom* and other such words that picture God's plans for His people. A beautiful word picture occurs, for example, in Psalm 85:10, where justice and peace (*shalom*) are said to have "kissed each other." *Shalom* reminds us God has mandated the right of each and every human being to flourish. Nicolas Wolterstorff has said it this way:

> God's love for justice is grounded in God's love for each and every one of God's human creatures. God's love for a human being consists of God desiring the good of that being–the good for a human being understood as the *shalom* of that human being. Justice consists of enjoying those goods, those components of one's shalom, to which one is morally entitled. So of course God loves justice and hates injustice.[9]

How does God sum up what God requires of His people? We are "to act justly and to love mercy and to walk humbly with [our] God" (Micah 6:8).

JESUS' KINGDOM OF SHALOM

We may expect the Old Testament, dealing with a nation and its neighbors, to stress practical, social matters. But some assume the New Testament message goes beyond, to more "spiritual" issues. Is this true?

Just as the creation story links God with the stuff of this earth, the incarnation of God's Son affirms God's love and concern for His creatures and the physical stuff we are made of. Jesus in the flesh identified with human hurts and suffering. He sanctifies by his own humanness the earthly concerns we deal with. Following Jesus along the paths of the Gospels, you see great acts of physical healing and compassion. You hear teachings on peacemaking and teachings cautioning that materialism, greed, injustice, and corruption lead only to death. Jesus displayed and advocated the holistic Good News in word, in sign, and in deed.

Jesus announced His ministry with the words of Isaiah the prophet, "The Spirit of the Lord is on me, because he has anointed me to preach good news to the poor...to proclaim freedom for the prisoners and recovery of sight for the blind, to release the oppressed, to proclaim the year of the Lord's favor" (Luke 4:18–19). Jesus' good news for the poor included *sign*—sight to the blind; it included *deed*—release for the oppressed; it included *word*—proclamation of the year of the Lord's favor. Having announced it, Jesus embarked on his mission, saying, "I must preach the good news of the kingdom of God to the other towns also, because that is why I was sent" (Luke 4:43).

Jesus' mysterious teaching of the Kingdom brings us closest to understanding the message of physical, social, and spiritual redemption and salvation. Yet, how can we talk about His Kingdom as present when Satan and the fruits of the Fall still exist? The same way Jesus did! Where He rules, the Kingdom is present. We preach the Kingdom, both "present" and "not yet." Where Jesus dwells and His people live, the Kingdom is present. Kingdom signs, words, and deeds abound. Abundant life, satisfaction, joy, reconciliation, hope, and peace rule. Ron Sider has said it this way, "Jesus' kingdom is clearly holistic. Thank God that it does bring forgiveness with God and personal, inner sanctification and power of the Spirit. But it also challenges and changes the social order."[10]

Preaching the Kingdom must be accompanied by the vibrant witness of the community of Christ's kingdom people. Preaching for social change is credible alongside the community of believers full of Jesus and His Spirit, living out His life in everyday deeds confirmed by His signs. Jesus called His followers salt and light, saying, "Let your light so shine before men that they may see your good deeds and praise your Father in heaven" (Matt. 5:16).

If we need convincing about helping tsunami and AIDS victims and their families, challenging the affluence and apathy of the church, or encouraging friendship and fellowship with inner city believers, we ought to hear once again Jesus' lesson on prayer. It hit home to me while listening to Jo Anne Lyon, founder and director of World Hope International, as she spoke to a college chapel audience on the wholeness of the Good News. "What did Jesus teach His disciples to pray?" she asked. "Thy Kingdom come, Thy will be done on *earth*, as it is in *heaven*." Christians rolling up their sleeves to help across the street and around the world can help to answer Jesus' kingdom prayer.

> Jesus' kingdom is clearly wholistic. Thank God that it does bring forgiveness with God and personal, inner sanctification and power of the Spirit. But it also challenges and changes the social order.
>
> —Ron Sider,
> *Good News and Good Works*

If we would preach a gospel that reflects Jesus, we must combine words and actions. The biblical story of God's plan and Jesus' message includes the whole package: justice, shalom, wholeness, reconciliation, and heart cleansing.

The world is watching and waiting to see Jesus in us. A missionary colleague of mine, Dr. Evvy Campbell, told of an incident during her time as a nurse at Kamakwie Wesleyan Hospital in Sierra Leone. A saintly African staff chaplain knocked on Evvy's door with a recently discharged woman in tow. Chaplain Memuna begged for some assistance to help the destitute patient return to her village. Evvy responded with a few clothing items, a towel, and some cash. Ya Memuna, who earlier had witnessed to the woman about Christ, danced with joy and exclaimed to her, "Look! Look good, because now you have seen Jesus!"

ACTION SUGGESTIONS

1. Connect with an inner-city or ethnically diverse group of believers. Make friends with the pastor and try to involve churches in mutual fellowship and service. Begin to see the world through the eyes of others.

2. Make service in the everyday world of need in your community a regular part of your own and your church's ministry. Encourage gifted members to tell their stories of Christ's love touching the hurting world.

3. Be widely informed. Don't confine your information gathering to one view, whether left or right, Christian or non-Christian. Make it a regular habit to view several networks for news—even the BBC, which often deals with global poverty and justice concerns that often are neglected stateside. Pick up magazines across a spectrum of viewpoints and be alert to where the world is hurting.

4. Preach through whole books in both the Old and the New Testament. You won't have to pick and choose favorite issues; the principles of God's heart for justice will emerge.

FOR FURTHER READING

Haugen, Gary. *Good News about Injustice: A Witness of Courage in a Hurting World.* Downers Grove: InterVarsity Press, 1999.

The "rest of the story" from Rwanda. Haugen's life work changed while investigating the genocide for the U.N. This primer clarifies the causes of injustice and offers practical steps for Christians, while telling about the birth of the International Justice Mission.

Lausanne Forum Reports 2004. "Holistic Mission." www.lausanne.org

This series of online reports on current issues includes the best evangelical thinking and theology from people who are doing the most with social concerns.

Lyon, Jo Anne. *The Ultimate Blessing: Rediscovering the Power of God's Presence*. Indianapolis: Wesleyan Publishing House, 2003.

A Wesleyan who put her faith into action tells her story and includes several chapters of powerful theory and practice of social justice and global compassion.

Perkins, John M. *Let Justice Roll Down*. Glendale: Regal Press, 1976.

Perkins has written newer books, but this respected evangelical leader's personal story of injustice and racism in America awakens us to an issue still plaguing the church.

Sider, Ronald J. *Good News and Good Works*. Grand Rapids: Baker Book House, 1993.

Perhaps the best evangelical holistic theology available, this is a biblical exploration of the relationship between evangelism and social concern.

Yamamori, Tetsunao, ed. *The Hope Factor: Engaging the Church in the HIV/AIDS Crisis*. Waynesboro, GA: Authentic Media, 2003.

Explains why the church with God's power has the potential to shift this worst of disasters into a turning point for hope in Africa and the world. This volume includes many authors and valuable case studies pastors ought to be familiar with.

NOTES

1. John Wesley, *The Character of a Methodist*, quoted in David D. Thompson, *John Wesley as a Social Reformer* (New York: Eaton and Mains, 1898), 26.

2. See John Wesley, *The Works of John Wesley* (Grand Rapids: Zondervan Publishing House, 1872 edition). Works of special interest in chronological order: 1745 "Appeal to Men of Reason" Vol. VIII, pp. 1–247; 1773 "Thoughts on the Present Scarcity of Provisions" Vol. XI: 53–59; 1774 "Thoughts Upon Slavery" Vol. XI. pp. 60–79; 1778 "A Serious Address to the People of England with Regard to the State of the Nation" Vol. XI: 140–149; 1782 "An Estimate of the Manners of the Present Time" Vol. XI: 156–164; 1782 "How Far is the Duty of the Christian

Minister to Preach Politics?" Vol. XI: 155; 1782 "A Plain account of the People Called Methodists" Vol. VIII: 248–268; others could be added to this list.

3. John Wesley, *Works*, Vol. XI, 70.

4. John Wesley, *The Letters of John Wesley*, Vol. VIII (London: The Epworth Press, 1931), 275.

5. Ibid., 276.

6. Ibid., 265.

7. John R. W. Stott, *The Contemporary Christian: Applying God's Word to Today's World* (Downers Grove: InterVarsity Press, 1992), 343.

8. John Steward, *Biblical Holism: Where God, People and Deeds Connect* (Burwood, Victoria: World Vision Australia, 1994), 11ff.

9. Nicholas Wolterstorff, "The God who Loves Justice and Our Love of the God Who Loves Justice," in the compendium, Justice and Global Witness (Washington: Council for Christian Colleges and Universities Workshop, 1999), 9.

10. Ronald J. Sider, *Good News and Good Works* (Grand Rapids: Baker Book House, 1993), 75.

WHO IS MY NEIGHBOR?

Cross-Cultural Preaching

Bill Peed

And who is my neighbor?

—Luke 10:29

The world is my parish.

—John Wesley

O n a hot afternoon in eastern Zambia, a new missionary was visiting the chief of his area who had become a Christian and joined the local Wesleyan church. As he prepared to leave, the chief inquired whether the missionary would visit one of his messengers who was sick. The missionary gladly agreed and walked with the local pastor about a kilometer to find the chief's messenger sitting underneath a large tree that provided plenty of shade from the afternoon sun. The messenger was suffering from bleeding gums and wanted prayer for healing. "What do I do?" the new missionary wondered. "I have no olive oil for anointing!"

Getting up from where he was sitting, the messenger walked over to his house, went inside, and returned with a small jar. The missionary unscrewed the lid and dipped his fingers into . . . Vaseline! Scooping out a generous portion, the missionary put the Vaseline on the Zambian brother's head and, in the name of the Lord, anointed him for healing.

As you may have guessed, I was that new missionary—and I had a lot to learn about the cultural differences that existed between Zambia and the United States. Around the world on a regular basis Wesleyan missionaries experience similar situations.

North American Wesleyan pastors increasingly find themselves in cross-cultural situations. They have not had to travel great distances to exotic locations for their cross-cultural encounters; diverse and interesting peoples have come to them. They may never have an experience quite like I did in Zambia, but they may have neighbors who are as culturally different from themselves as I was from the Zambian chief's sick messenger. To preach effectively to our ethnically diverse neighbors, we have to learn to present both the gospel and ourselves in ways our listeners can understand.

Wesley's perspective that the whole world was his parish encompasses love for every person in the local, multi-cultural congregation. Such love will be lived out through a desire to preach well cross-culturally—telling the good news of Jesus Christ to people who contrast culturally with the preacher, in areas like language, ethnic background, social status, and religious beliefs—whether near or abroad.

At the time of this writing, Wesleyans in the United States and Canada minister in over 240 Native American, African-American, Hispanic, Asian, and multi-ethnic churches.[1] Many people represented by these numbers are shepherded by Wesleyan pastors whose cultural backgrounds differ from the people in their congregations.

In the year 2000, almost thirteen percent of the population in the United States was Hispanic, making it the largest minority in the country. That is projected to increase to over twenty-four percent, almost 103 million people, by the year 2050.[2] Statistics can be helpful, but they become more meaningful when we connect faces to the numbers. It's like meeting a next-door neighbor; when we make the effort to relate a numerical finding to a national family, we become more deeply aware of their fascinating *diversity*. As we begin to feel their *different-ness*, we must ask, "How do we preach with competence to these folk?" To be effective cross-cultural preachers, we Wesleyans need to examine our attitudes and our preaching perspectives, both of which play powerful roles in our communication of the gospel.

THE ATTITUDE OF ETHNOCENTRISM

Nearly a hundred years ago, a word was coined to describe the practice of holding to a set of beliefs to the extent that they were judged to be superior to another set of beliefs.[3] This word is ethnocentrism. Ethnocentrism today is assuming the intrinsic superiority of a specific ethnic group or culture (usually one's own).

All of us tend to believe that the things we do, the values we hold, and the ways we think are right; otherwise, we wouldn't do them. Ethnocentrism in and of itself is not a bad thing—it is a sign of confident group-esteem. This self-love becomes harmful only when it causes us to treat other groups poorly, when it blinds us to the different, but certainly not wrong, customs of other cultures, turning us into cultural imperialists. As Jesus said, "Why do you look at the speck of sawdust in your brother's eye and pay no attention to the plank in your own eye?" (Matt. 7:3).

Ethnocentrism "weaves its way into thoughts and actions, such as arrogance, avoidance, withdrawal, faulty attribution, and faulty categorizing."[4] Here is a short exercise to help you determine whether ethnocentrism negatively affects your life. For each of the five statements, rate yourself between 1 and 5, 1 meaning, "I highly agree," and 5 meaning "I highly disagree."

1. Generally speaking, the way things are done in my hometown is the best way for most other places as well.

2. Foreigners have a responsibility to learn local customs when they come to my country.

3. The rapid influx of immigrants into my country will ruin it eventually.

4. It would be better if English were spoken as a universal language.

5. People from my country tend to be smarter than people from most other places.[5]

So, how did you do? The higher your score, the lower your ethnocentrism.

Ethnocentrism reveals itself in many ways; examples are prejudice against ethnic minorities, bigotry (narrow-mindedness or intolerance of others who are different), and racism. It further manifests itself in those who find it difficult to build relationships with those outside their own racial or ethnic group—or even social clique. Wesleyan preachers express ethnocentrism when we hold on to styles of worship, preaching, and discipleship that are comfortable for us but foreign to our cross-cultural congregations. When we recognize our ethnocentric tendencies and control these tendencies, we move toward greater effectiveness in our cross-cultural preaching.

> One of the greatest stumbling blocks to understanding other peoples within or without a particular culture is the tendency to judge others' behaviors by our own standards.
>
> —James Down

THEMES IN CROSS-CULTURAL UNDERSTANDING

One of the few extensive research studies into cross-cultural preaching was conducted in 2001 by James Nieman and Thomas Rogers.[6] Homiletics teachers and cross-cultural preachers themselves, Nieman and Rogers interviewed over seventy ministers from large, small, rural, urban, and suburban churches of various denominations spread across the United States who were involved on a weekly basis with Native American, Hispanic, Latino, and Asian peoples. (African-Americans were not included in the target group, though several were interviewed.)

As Nieman and Rogers analyzed their data, they discovered four broad themes related to cross-cultural preaching: ethnicity, class, displacement, and beliefs. Cultural differences became most visible when considered in light of these themes. Nieman and Rogers then suggested group characteristics and preaching strategies for each.

ETHNICITY

When Nieman and Rogers speak of ethnicity in this context, they are not referring to race but to the peoples of a specific country. This means, for example, that to speak of Hispanics in terms of race is to refer broadly to people of Spain or Spanish-speaking countries of the Americas. On the other hand, when speaking of Hispanics in terms of ethnicity, one is referring to the people, or peoples, of specific countries, such as Mexico, Venezuela, or Chile. People usually find belonging and meaning in life more broadly through their specific country of origin than through their racial descent.

Every ethnic group bases its interactions on fundamental relationships of trust. Often these interactions are coded in speech patterns, genres, and sayings that are beyond the understanding of the uninitiated outsider. When the background of the preacher is radically different from that of the congregation, his or her vocation/avocation is to learn as much as possible about them. (This can be true even if the preacher and the congregation speak the same language. By Nieman and Rogers's definition of ethnicity, the United States comprises numerous distinct ethnic groups, most of whom also speak English.)

> When I'm referring to identity in a sermon for a Hispanic group, somehow I have to bring in the family theme or some family focus there, because that's what our identity's based on.
>
> —Nieman and Rogers,
> *Preaching to Every Pew:*
> *Cross-Cultural Strategies*

Within each ethnic group exist subgroups. Differences between some ethnic subgroups may contribute to strong and obvious, even violent, tensions between those groups. The cross-cultural preacher must recognize these tensions as realities affecting the congregation.

The preacher also needs to determine the core values, characteristics, attitudes, and ideals for which the ethnic group is clearly known—things like knowing the status of the sacred scriptures of the group's dominant religion or recognizing the religious leader(s) in the ethnic group. Taking the time to discover these facts will enhance the effectiveness of the cross-cultural preacher.

As cross-cultural preachers we can incorporate a variety of practices into our preaching strategy to increase the chances of being effective: using expressions that are meaningful to that ethnic group; learning the language; decorating the home with ethnic art; playing (and enjoying!) ethnic music.

CLASS

Understanding class is another way cross-cultural preachers can preach with effectiveness. In this context, class refers to the status of a person within the group, to one's station in life. Often we in the

West associate class with educational achievement or economic success. However, in the setting of cross-cultural preaching, class also refers to realities like social caste, group affiliation, status within a family, and religious membership. As cross-cultural preachers we need to keep in mind the realities of class that affect our congregants and how their class backgrounds directly or indirectly shape their present-day situations.

Within each ethnic group exist several classes, even subclasses. To be relevant to the needs of a cross-cultural congregation, we need to identify these subclasses. These different classes may perceive the preacher differently, giving us a higher or lower status depending on their own status. Being aware of this helps us relate to each person accordingly.

How a group processes *what they hear* is clearly influenced by the class to which they belong. Those who hear us use words like security, hope, power, holiness, grace, and blessing in a sermon very well may interpret those words differently from how we intended. Each of these group characteristics should influence the strategy we use for crafting our sermons.

As we create our sermons for cross-cultural congregations, we will do well to consider several strategic questions: Does this message address the ordinary happenings of daily existence (such as neighborhood realities) rather than being abstract in content and focus? Do I give my cross-cultural hearers, some of whom may come from oral societies, numerous opportunities throughout the message to hear the point(s) I am making? Do the specific texts I chose for this

> By virtue of the pastor/people relationship, they have increasingly granted me more authority as a preacher. They have sensed that I deeply and genuinely care for them, and they for me.
>
> —Nieman and Rogers,
> *Preaching to Every Pew:*
> *Cross-Cultural Strategies*

message point my hearers toward a vision of God's liberating hope in the midst of their class realities?

DISPLACEMENT

The quandary of how to anoint the chief's messenger for healing that day in Zambia was neither the first nor the last drama I experienced in this culture far removed from my home setting. Culture shock happens to anyone—missionary, immigrant, cross-cultural preacher, student, even tourist—who crosses from one culture to another for any extended period of time. If left unexamined and unresolved, the effects of culture shock may adversely affect an individual or an entire family for many years.

> The preacher's central task [in confronting displacement] is to assist people in rebuilding a culture.
>
> —Nieman and Rogers,
> *Preaching to Every Pew:*
> *Cross-Cultural Strategies*

For people immigrating to another country, culture shock can be tremendously unsettling and disorienting. Generally, when newcomers arrive they are overwhelmed with the realization that the new culture is frustratingly *different*. As time progresses, the inequities brought on by biases (real or imagined) can combine to produce a way of life dominated by isolation and alienation from those who are seen to be the shapers and power brokers of the culture.

Nieman and Rogers chose the word "displacement" to discuss what happens when people experience a "movement or shift away from a customary setting."[7] Displacement is the compelling idea that people, when uprooted from their original cultural setting, lose most if not all the steady anchors in their lives. The cross-cultural preacher must understand the powerful effects of displacement on the congregation and choose effective strategies to counteract its negative influences.

To a large extent displacement is an invisible, under-the-surface reality for immigrants. It is analogous to an inner, bodily wound; no one sees it, but it is real and painful. Displacement may reveal itself when people talk in detail about leaving their home cultures to come to another. For some, that journey is very costly emotionally as well as socially. Displacement comes to the surface when people talk about the dynamics of generational bonds between group members and how that affects how they relate to those outside their group.

It is possible to preach effectively to those experiencing displacement. For example, we can use words that are both deeply profound and easily identifiable. If we preach in English, we need to speak at an appropriate speed for those whose first language is not English. The imageries we use in our preaching ought to communicate clear word pictures that encourage sincere responses. Genesis 12, Matthew 15, Luke 10, and John 4 are potent examples of such imagery. Displacement is eased when themes of lament are addressed directly rather than being sugar-coated. Seeing the sermon as a beginning or continuing point in the ongoing conversation about life helps to sand down the hard edges of displacement.

BELIEFS

Diverse peoples in our congregations bring their unique cultural backgrounds with them to church. These backgrounds may include a religion other than Christianity. When merged in a church of different ethnicities, these histories create a rich tapestry of religious understandings.

The astute cross-cultural preacher will realize the importance and necessity of dialogue with others of differing religious beliefs. By looking at the characteristics of these beliefs, we understand the congregation more fully and preach the gospel more effectively.

Beliefs are intertwined in the fabric of the ordinary life. Cross-cultural preaching identifies ordinary behaviors associated with these beliefs. For example, what beliefs drive particular behaviors of Hindus, who have no problem adding Christ as another deity to be worshipped to their already innumerable number of gods?

> So much of the preaching that's appreciated and responded to here . . . rarely takes place on Sundays.
>
> —Nieman and Rogers, *Preaching to Every Pew: Cross-Cultural Strategies*

The way we express religious beliefs can create barriers that make communication across religions difficult. The challenge in cross-cultural preaching is to lessen the barrier without compromising the message. At times, the truth of the Christian message will provide a starting point for building trust with those of other religions. For example, Wesleyans believe the gospel has social implications. Involvement in community organizations like the PTA and scouting, in relief and development work, or church-sponsored English classes helps open doors to hearts that may otherwise be closed to our message.

Regular practices in and outside the pulpit can help us grasp more deeply, from a cross-cultural perspective, the beliefs of others. One way to do this is to separate the essentials that Wesleyans hold to be biblically true from behaviors that may be more culturally based. Knowing how to articulate basic Christian beliefs, clearly and lovingly, to those of other religions helps to foster effective cross-cultural preaching.

Remember the Vaseline story? That was a powerful "Aha!" moment for me. I began to appreciate more than ever before a paradigm-shifting truth: The form of the gospel (in this case, Vaseline) *must* change across cultures if it is to bear fruit, but the function of the gospel (healing in and through Christ's name) must never change.

Perhaps some paradigms in our cross-cultural preaching need to be shifted or replaced. Perhaps we have communicated the function of the gospel less effectively because we have not changed its form. Let us all be encouraged to examine our ethnocentrism and review our parishes, their memberships, and their cultural habits, through the frames of ethnicity, class, displacement, and beliefs. After all, increased effectiveness in our cross-cultural preaching is God's mandate for our day.

ACTION SUGGESTIONS

1. What tendencies do you see in yourself toward ethnocentrism? List three behaviors you are willing to change in yourself to become a global communicator of the gospel.

2. Write down four or five ethnic sayings understood by the cross-cultural members of your congregation, sayings you think could create stronger bonds between you and them if you were to use them in your preaching.

3. Think about the sermons you've preached over the last three to six months. How often have they been embedded in the ordinary experiences of life? What changes could you make in your messages so they could speak to the specific community issues of the people who attend your cross-cultural church?

4. Use your visits with the cross-cultural members of your congregation as opportunities to follow through on the messages you have preached, so your hearers can engage them more deeply and have greater opportunity to move beyond their feelings of displacement.

5. Effective cross-cultural preaching engages other religious beliefs as well as declares the truth of Scripture. Identify two or three things you could do to initiate and promote dialogue with other religious leaders in your community.

FOR FURTHER READING

Dodd, Carley H. *Dynamics of Intercultural Communication.* Boston: McGraw Hill, 1998.

Dodd's text covers broadly the study of intercultural communications, and is helpful in understanding many topics related to the field.

Elmer, Duane H. *Cross-Cultural Connections: Stepping Out and Fitting In Around the World.* Downers Grove: InterVarsity Press, 2002.

Although focused more for use in settings outside North America, Elmer's book will greatly assist those ministering in the North American cross-cultural setting, as well, since it contains many helpful insights into cross-cultural ministry.

Nieman, James R. and **Rogers**, Thomas G. *Preaching to Every Pew: Cross-Cultural Strategies.* Minneapolis: Fortress Press, 2001.

This book is perhaps the only one on the market today focusing solely on cross-cultural preaching in the United States; it will be an excellent resource for your library.

Spencer, Aida and William. *The Global God: Multicultural Evangelical Views of God.* Grand Rapids: Baker Book House, 1998.

The Spencers have compiled a valuable resource for those with multiple ethnic groups represented in their congregations. Each chapter is written by an international representing a view of God from his/her part of the world, helping readers understand perspectives about God from a multi-cultural perspective.

NOTES

1. Joseph Watkins, E-mail letter from Joe Watkins to Bill Peed, 27 January 2005.

2. U. S. Census Bureau, *U. S. Interim Projections by Age, Sex, Race, and Hispanic Origin* (2004) <www.census.gov/ipc/www/usinterimproj/natprojtab01a.pdf>.

3. William G. Sumner, *Folkways: A Study of the Sociological Importance of Usages, Manners, Customs, and Morals* (Boston: Ginn, 1906).

4. Carley H. Dodd, *Dynamics of Intercultural Communication*. 5th ed. (Boston: McGraw-Hill, 1998).

5. Kregg Hood, "Ethnocentrism Measure," *Dynamics of Intercultural Communication*. 5th ed. (Boston: McGraw-Hill, 1998), 266.

6. James R. Nieman and Thomas G. Rogers, *Preaching to Every Pew: Cross-Cultural Strategies* (Minneapolis: Fortress, 2001).

7. Ibid., 85.

11

WHAT DO THEY WANT?

The Practice of Preaching

Jo Anne Lyon

The Lord God has given me the tongue of those who are taught, that I may know how to sustain with a word those that are weary. Morning by morning God wakens my ear to hear as those who are taught.

—Isaiah 50:4

The trials which a gracious Providence sends, may be precious means of growing in grace, and particularly of increasing in faith [and] patience.

—John Wesley, Letter to Miss Hester Ann Roe, October 6, 1776

D ixie is an excellent psychotherapist trained in the Graduate School of Social Work of Washington University. All week long she works with some of the most desperate people of St. Louis, Missouri. Her professional skills coupled with her passion for healing is evidenced by the many people who have entered her door and now are living with hope.

During one of our monthly accountability breakfasts she leaned across the table and said, in near confidential tones, "I am so hungry to hear biblical preaching that feeds my soul deep within." Feeling more comfortable, she leaned back and said, "Frankly I am tired of preachers who try to be psychologists and, generally, not very well." We both laughed, probably too smugly for our own good.

As we began to discuss her statement in more detail, I asked if she just wanted straight Bible teaching as in a classroom. "No, I need more than that," she said thoughtfully. "I need more than just information. I need something to touch my spirit and give me new life."

LIVING AMONG THE PEOPLE

We need to rediscover the mystery of the Holy Spirit reaching us at deep levels through preaching. Henri Nouwen has noted that pastors and preaching have been marginalized by the experts. In other words, every issue in life has a specialist. We have blurred the spiritual with all these experts and have relegated preaching either to a form of nice speaking or to mere entertainment.[1]

This is not a new issue. It is centuries old. The people who listened to Jesus preach noted that something was different. In a number of places the Gospels note that Jesus taught like no one they had ever heard. His parables are wonderful examples of truths taught by using familiar events in His listeners' lives. It is imperative to note that Jesus lived out His teaching and preaching. Jesus was not competing in His style and delivery with any nearby rabbi. He was giving His life so the people would believe.

The order we know today as the Dominicans was set aside as the Order of Preachers in A.D. 1220. Their purpose was to teach and preach. They called for an educated clergy able to communicate with the people through sermons. Their sermons were marked by humor as well as by rhyme and stories from everyday life. They wrote devotional books, essentially paraphrases of Scripture in local languages, as well as religious poetry. But their greatest calling was "to live among the people."[2]

LISTENING

Living among the people means *listening* to them. What are their life stories? Generally these are stories they have believed about themselves since childhood and have lived out as they've seen them scripted. The claim of the gospel, however, is that a new redemptive story at the margins is begging to break through, if only they will notice and respond. Preaching can be the means by which this new life bursts forth into the consciousness of the hearer. Many times we have shifted this emphasis to small groups or support groups while marginalizing the preaching event as pretty speeches in a corporate setting rather than allowing it to function as the Holy-Spirit-anointed, living Word of God breaking into people's lives.

> A leader OF the Word is essentially a leader TO the Word.
>
> —Basil the Great

Listening to people also means listening to what they are listening to. What music shapes them? What do they watch on TV? What Internet sites do they frequent? Who are their heroes? What radio stations are their favorites? What books do they read? All these are powerful influences in defining and shaping people's stories. This knowledge can become a bridge to the relevance of the gospel.

In this postmodern era, increasing numbers of preachers are using clips from contemporary movies, music, plays, and poetry to bridge this gap very effectively. The danger is that the movie clips can become the strongest part of the sermon. On occasion, listeners go home and dig up the movie to watch it again, but can't remember the link to the Scriptures or the sermon. Keeping in mind that preaching is moving people toward transformation should help focus the strength and power of the Scriptures in the sermon.

TRANSPARENCY

Living among the people is a vulnerable place for the preacher because it calls for appropriate levels of *transparency*. By this, I don't mean preaching as a one-way litany of disappointments and personal foibles dumped on the congregation by the preacher. Rather, appropriate transparency can bring reality to preaching because most preachers are looking for hope from their own preaching.

Henri Nouwen discusses this appropriate transparency as evidenced in a different setting:

> It is not just curiosity which makes people listen to a preacher when he or she speaks directly to a man and woman whose marriage is being blessed or to the children of the man who has just been buried in the ground. They listen in the deep-seated hope that a personal concern might give the preacher words that carry beyond the ears of those whose joy or suffering he/she shares. Few listen to a sermon which is intended to be applicable to everyone, but most pay careful attention to words born out of concern for only a few. . . . All this suggests that when one has the courage to enter where life is experienced as most unique and most private, one touches the soul of the community.[3]

ACCOUNTABILITY

Living among the people should bring *accountability*. Our preaching should reflect the life and passion of the preacher and the community. The current information culture has created an extensive atmosphere of preaching competition, regularly tempting us to find our way to the Internet to find well-constructed sermons by currently popular preachers. These may or may not be the "word of the Lord" for this congregation. More to the point, are they—can they be—connected to our own soul if they are not our own sermons? We must also ask, "Is this what I am living as well as preaching?"

John Wesley eschewed such preacherly competition. In the *Preface to the Sermons*, he wrote:

I design plain truth for plain people...I abstain from all the nice and philosophical speculations...I labor to avoid all words which are not easy to be understood, all of which are not used in common life and in particular, those kinds of technical terms that so frequently occur in Bodies of Divinity...but which to common people are an unknown tongue. Yet, I am not assured, that I do not slide into them unawares; it is so extremely natural to imagine that a word which is familiar to ourselves is so to all the world."[4]

Here we find Wesley in touch with the lives of the people to whom he preached, resisting the great sermon oratorical competition of his day. So passionate was Wesley in his preaching that he and George Whitefield were forced from the church pulpits to the streets and fields. Their preaching struck at the heart of

> The preaching of the Gospel does not demand that I decide for Christ. It invites me to live in the decision that God in Christ has made for me. The preaching of the Gospel does not persuade me to make up my mind. It woos me to give up my heart.
>
> —Lowell Erdahl

comfortable economic life in England at that time, particularly over the issue of slavery. As a result, the alienated poor were recaptured for the church. Not only slavery, but the issues of fair prices, a living wage, and honest, healthy employment for all were part of their call to holy living. Richard Lovelace states, "The Wesleyan movement set in motion the grassroots awakening which provided a broad popular base for the social achievements of the Second and Third Awakenings in England during the nineteenth century."[5]

The preaching of John Wesley regarding these issues was not "political preaching," as some would call it today. Rather, it was a "voice for the voiceless," as were the sermons of the Old Testament Prophets and Jesus. This was preaching about justice, not about favoring a particular political party. Preaching about issues of justice is difficult and treads a fine line, especially since it seems the more popular preaching in our culture is about reaching one's potential for achievement. However, people will respond to passionate preaching about justice if we can help them see it as derived from Scripture and related to the kingdom of God on earth. Our justice preaching cannot be a few favorite topics. By this I mean the passion of preaching about godly marriages should be equaled by the passion of preaching on the sin of racism. The topic of caring for God's creation should be at least as vital in our preaching as is the topic of same-sex marriages.

> When one has the courage to enter where life is experienced as most unique and most private, one touches the soul of the community.
>
> —Henri Nouwen,
> *The Wounded Healer*

Preaching on justice issues is part of leading people in their spiritual formation. Justice and moral issues are present in most texts. One need not be unduly inventive to see a real relationship, not a forced one, between what is written on the sacred page and a factory closing, a brutal murder, a tense educational situation—the events go on.

Questions can assist in making these connections: What specific ethical questions are raised by this scriptural passage? What are relevant ethical principles, teachings, or virtues? How am I using Scripture as a moral source? As a moral reminder? As a moral analogy? As a command of God? How does this scriptural word speak to or illuminate the moral values to be sought?

More than one billion people live on less than a dollar a day, and over twenty-five thousand die daily due to lack of clean drinking water. This is cause for justice preaching. Jonathan Edwards wrote in 1746, "The proliferation of religiosity in the form of meetings for prayer, singing and religious talk will not promote or sustain revival without works of love and mercy, which will bring the God of love down from heaven to earth...to set up his tabernacle with men on the earth, and dwell with them."[6] He went on to say,

> Experiences of renewal which are genuinely from the Holy Spirit are God-centered in character, based on worship, an appreciation of God's worth and grandeur divorced from self-interest. Such experiences create humility in the convert rather than pride and issue in the creation of a new spirit of meekness, gentleness, forgiveness and mercy. They leave the believer hungering and thirsting after righteousness instead of satiated with self-congratulation. Most important their end result is the performance of works of mercy and justice.[7]

The First, Second, and Third Awakenings were spawned through prayer and preaching; the result was social reform. This was not done through one sermon, but by the continual practice of preaching. It is interesting to note that no effective social witness has happened throughout history without a revived church.[8]

THE PRACTICE OF PREACHING

What is the *practice* of preaching? Perhaps it will help to think of preaching as analogous to the *practice* of medicine by a physician or the *practice* of law by an attorney. If we consider preaching to be, in some respects, on a par with medicine or law, we will see the critical imperative of our continued research (continuing education) in many areas—the meaning of Scripture, the means of delivery, the culture(s) addressed, and others.

KNOWING OUR HEARERS

The *practice* of preaching involves using different styles and approaches appropriate to the variety of hearers we address. Some learn visually, others through logical sequence, still others through narrative or storytelling. Thomas Long says, "When we create a sermon form we are not primarily asking, 'What is the most orderly way for this material to fit together?' We are rather asking, 'How can people best *hear* the material in this sermon?' . . . A sermon form is a plan for the experience of listening."[9]

> Experiences of renewal which are genuinely from the Holy Spirit are God-centered . . . .. Most important their end result is the performance of works of mercy and justice.
>
> —Jonathan Edwards, *A Treatise on Religious Affections*

GENDER-INCLUSIVE PREACHING

Jesus knew His *hearers* and used the common threads and experiences of their lives to teach the basic principles of the kingdom of God. He used both male and female life experiences in His parables. This was radical in an era when women were regarded as of little value. By doing this, Jesus made clear that women as well as men are part of the kingdom of God.

By contrast, in this twenty-first century, Robert Howard noted that the first five sermons in one issue of *Pulpit Digest* contained twenty-four images used by the preachers. Twenty of the twenty-four images used only men as examples; two others portrayed both men and women as actors; only two portrayed only women in active roles. Howard concluded, "Theologically, the exclusion of women's point of view in the imagery of sermons distorts the very Good News that preachers seek to proclaim."[10]

Alice Matthews illustrates this truth:

Women who do not know that they can take action to change bad situations do well to hear of Abigail (1 Samuel 25). She was married to an evil man, Nabal, who acted stupidly toward those to whom he had a debt. When his actions provoked David to organize a full-scale military action against Nabal's household, quick-thinking Abigail headed off the trouble that threatened the lives of everyone under her roof. In going against her husband's wishes, she saved his life. She changed a stressful situation rather than merely wringing her hands about it.[11]

One more illustration from Matthews may nail down our point here:

The story of Leah (Genesis 29–30) [portrays] a woman married to a man who did not love her. Watch her do everything in her power (unsuccessfully) to earn her husband's love. But also look at the progression in her mind and heart as she named her six sons. This woman could not change her stressful situation, but she could change the meaning of it as she came to focus not on what she lacked (Jacob's love) but on what God had given her (six sons). She could be psychologically whole even without the love of her husband. It is difficult to name many problems people face today that were not faced and overcome by women in the biblical narratives.[12]

Clearly, the principles of these situations apply to both men and women. Yet, it is empowering for women to hear these principles from the experiences of their own gender, as Jesus' preaching allowed them to do two thousand years ago.

DWELLING IN THE STORY

Both Abigail's and Leah's narratives model the use of story in preaching. The hearer can integrate the biblical story and his or her personal story, and a new story of healing and wholeness emerges. Henri Nouwen said, "One of the remarkable qualities of the story is that it creates space. We can dwell in a story, walk around, find our own place. The story confronts but does not oppress; the story inspires but does not manipulate. The story invites us to an encounter, a dialog, a mutual sharing."[13] Story helps us to come in touch with God's Story, My Story, and Our (Community of Believers) Story.

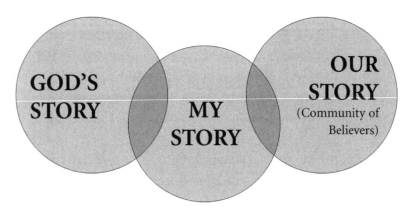

The three functional questions for sermon preparation discussed and used by many today are: What does the text mean? Is it true? So what? Many sermons stop with the attempt to answer the first question, creating passive listeners. The second question brings the hearer to a thinking mode, which is a prerequisite for the third question in which the hearer begins to integrate his or her reality with the ideal that has been presented. The use of story in preaching can be a very effective strategem because the listener wrestles with the text through the story while at the same time integrating his or her own story into God's story.

Again, Nouwen reminds us:

> The rabbis guide their people with stories; ministers usually guide with ideas and theories. We need to become storytellers again, and so multiply our ministry by calling around us the great witnesses who in different ways offer guidance to doubting hearts. A story that guides is a story that opens a door and offers us space in which to search and boundaries to help us find what we seek, but it does not tell us what to do or how to do it. As long as we have stories to tell to each other there is hope.[14]

USING ALL THE TOOLS

In the twenty-first century, we have a plethora of means available for telling the story. One approach is to create ways to engage all the senses in hearing and experiencing the story. For example, this can be done through music, multisensory elements, hands-on illustrations, art forms, liturgical movements, interactive forums, drama, film, and other visual media—and even through simple, honest sharing.

All this is engaging in the *practice* of preaching. As the lawyer no longer has an assistant taking shorthand on a pad of paper but has moved to the technology of the computer, so the preacher moves to the methods of this generation. However, we must be careful to ensure that the methods do not override the message. The attorney still needs to know the law, after all.

Another powerful preaching tool is metaphor. For warrant, we need only look to Scripture itself; virtually every page is saturated with metaphors and similes. The books of Isaiah and Amos, and virtually all of Jesus' preaching, are only a few examples.

An apt metaphor allows and helps listeners take the theme of the scripture passage and apply it creatively to their own situation. For example, the metaphor of a light bulb in the context of Jesus' teaching that He is the light of the world can introduce many stimulating thoughts. We have the power to turn the electric light bulb off and on at will. Would Jesus ever turn off the light? Can we turn off Jesus' light in our lives? The questions easily could continue.

PREACHING TO DIXIE NOW

Dixie and I no longer meet for breakfast. Our lives have taken several turns and I have moved some twelve hundred miles to the east. Dixie's successful career as a psychotherapist has been interrupted by a shocking disability. She is now confined to a wheel chair with ALS (Lou Gehrig's disease).

When I asked her recently how her faith has survived such a terrible adversity, she made it clear how important it is for preachers to address the second question (Is it true?). She began talking about the gap between what one is taught and what one truly believes. "The sovereignty of God needs to be nailed down *before* you get into these unexplainable situations," she said firmly. With a break in her voice she said, "I can't explain it all, but I experience God picking me up and loving me."

That pressed me to find out more about what she expects from a sermon. "I [still] need to hear biblical preaching that makes me think and how it applies to my life at this time," she told me. I assumed that in her condition, passion and cultural engagement no longer were a part of her needs in preaching. But I was quite wrong. "Absolutely, we must be in community and be grace-givers; and this comes with passion. In fact," she continued, "my years working for Catholic Charities has influenced me [to think] that preaching is almost sacramental. The preacher is representing God to the people, and God's truth goes through him or her to the people. When that happens it is quite passionate."

> We need to become story-tellers again . . . .. As long as we have stories to tell each other there is hope.
>
> —Henri Nouwen,
> *The Living Reminder*

The words of the prophet Amos ring out today. The Lord says there will be "not a famine of bread, nor a thirst for water, but of hearing the words of the Lord" (Amos 8:11). God's people are hungry and thirsting for God's Word, and they are taking to their feet in search of it.

With the call to preach comes Isaiah's reminder, "The Lord God has given me the tongue of those who are taught, that I may know how to sustain with a word those that are weary. Morning by morning God wakens my ear to hear as those who are taught" (Isa. 50:4). The opening of self to the power of the Most High lets the Holy Spirit overshadow the preacher. The seed of God's truth and love present in the Word is planted in faith.

One final note. Since the writing of this chapter, Dixie now is fully living into all the preaching that sustained her in her final months. She began her celebration with our Lord in July 2005.

ACTION SUGGESTIONS

1. Consider these and similar questions when approaching any text you are thinking of preaching: What moved, inspired, challenged, encouraged, consoled, or even provoked you in this passage? What visual images does this passage evoke for you? What connections did you make between this passage and your personal experience? Between this passage and your local community? Between this passage and the world community? Did any words, phrases, or sentences in this passage puzzle you?

2. Consider beginning a weekly meeting of staff or lay people to discuss and ask questions about the scripture passage for the upcoming Sunday. Hearing other's ideas and questions often can stimulate a direction for the preacher. In addition, you and the other worship leaders can identify media and other creative means for communicating the text.

3. Invite the congregation to schedule faith-sharing sessions after your sermons, over coffee or tea, without the preacher present. The discussion questions would be, "How did God's word through the sermon reach me/us today? What difference will it make in my/our week?"

A facilitator could be responsible to give the preacher a tape or notes of the discussion so the preacher can discover whether he or she has been heard and understood. This process has been noted to strengthen both the hearers and the preacher.

FOR FURTHER READING

Brueggemann, Walter. *Texts under Negotiation: The Bible and Postmodern Imagination.* Minneapolis: Fortress Press, 1993.

Brueggemann has chosen six Old Testament texts to illustrate how they can be preached/presented as relevant to the postmodern situation.

Buttrick, David. *Homiletic: Moves and Structures*. Philadelphia: Fortress Press, 1987.

The preaching style of "moves" as opposed to "outline" is aimed to fit with the experience of listening. The goal of this rhetorical form is to shape the preacher's, and the text's, "moves" to fit human consciousness. Ideally, people should not feel they are being talked to as much as they experience having the text's conceptual meaning form in their own consciousness as their own process.

Matthews, Alice P. *Preaching that Speaks to Women*. Grand Rapids: Baker Academic, 2003.

This eye-opening book discusses the preaching event as having taken women for granted. It is filled with practical methods by which to rectify the gap in communication. Haddon Robinson states in his introduction, "The women who sit before us are not our grandmothers' generation. They want to be treated as Christians who possess all the Spirit's gifts and not as second-rate citizens of the kingdom. If we Christian leaders ignore them, we do so to our peril and theirs."

NOTES

1. Henri Nouwen, *In the Name of Jesus* (New York: Crossroad Press, 1995), 19–21.

2. Tim Dowley, Ed., *Eerdmans' Handbook to the History of Christianity* (Grand Rapids: Wm. B. Eerdmans, 1977), 263.

3. Henri Nouwen, *The Wounded Healer* (New York: Doubleday, 1972), quoted in *A Guide to Prayer for Ministers and Other Servants* (Nashville: The Upper Room, 1983), 200.

4. Edward H. Sugden, *Wesley's Standard Sermons*, Volume 1 (Grand Rapids: Francis Asbury Press, 1955), 30.

5. Richard F. Lovelace, *Dynamics of Spiritual Life* (Downers Grove: InterVarsity Press, 1979), 370.

6. Ibid., 43.

7. Ibid., 42.

8. Ibid., 377.

9. Thomas G. Long, *The Witness of Preaching* (Louisville: Westminster/John Knox Press, 1989), 96.

10. Robert Howard, "Gender and Point of View in the Imagery of Preaching," *Pulpit Digest* (Jan/Feb 1991): 5.

11. Alice P. Mathews, *Preaching that Speaks to Women* (Grand Rapids: Baker Academic, 2003), 61.

12. Ibid, 62.

13. Henri J. Nouwen, *The Living Reminder* (New York: Seabury Press, 1977), quoted in *A Guide to Prayer for Ministers and Other Servants* (Nashville: The Upper Room, 1983), 247.

14. Ibid.

THE POWER OF A MOMENT

The Verdict

David Eaton

On Sunday morning when the bells ring to call the congregation and minister to worship, there is in the air an expectancy that something great, crucial, and momentous is to happen . . . . 'God is present! God is present.'

—Karl Barth, *The Word of God and the Word of Man*

[T]he first principle of Methodism . . . [is] wholly and solely to preach the Gospel. . . . [P]roclaim to all the world the lovingkindness of God our Saviour.

—John Wesley, Sermon CXV, "The Ministerial Office"

Following a Sunday morning service about thirty years ago, I was happily greeting the church folks—but their usual "Good sermon, Pastor" comments were missing. Things got worse when up walked 92-year-old Walter Ward and he gave me his evaluation. It wasn't good news. Mr. Ward stood less than five feet tall, but he looked up at my six-foot-three-inch frame and let me have it. "Preacher," he said. "I didn't understand a word of your sermon."

This experience led me to consider more seriously the purpose of the sermon. Over the intervening years I have concluded that the preaching moment is a means of grace for the transformation of listeners' lives by the grace and power of God.

I've been privileged to be a part of that. In one of my pastorates a young man in his early twenties started coming to church because of his interest in Sharon, an attractive young Christian woman. I was very disappointed when I learned Rick was not a Christian but was from a very pagan background. Even so, and to the credit of the congregation, Rick received a consistently warm welcome as he dated Sharon.

> And what is preaching for? The answer comes without hesitation. It is for men's salvation.
>
> —Phillips Brooks, *Lectures on Preaching*

Suddenly, one day, Rick disappeared. No one in the church, not even Sharon, knew where he was. The mystery of his disappearance continued for about two weeks, as did our apprehension. Then, as suddenly as he had disappeared, Rick reappeared.

Rick explained that after he started coming to church he felt something he had never experienced before. He said, "When I came to church I felt warmth and a presence I didn't understand. I began to feel miserable inside. I decided to take a trip. I traveled from place to place wondering what was wrong with me." He explained how the fellowship of the church, the presence of God, and the preaching of the Word had awakened him to his inner need. Shortly after his return, Rick gave his heart to the Lord. Later, Rick and Sharon were married and established a fine Christian family. God used the power of the preaching moment, among other things, to draw Rick into God's family.

THE POWER OF THE *KAIROS*

Every sermon faithful to its biblical sources and communicated through a Spirit-led preacher is a grace-filled *kairos* moment. When scriptural truth is spoken with careful preparation, humble love, and God's passionate anointing the powers of heaven are marshaled in the frontal assault on the principalities and powers of this world. And the battleground is the heart of the hearer.

Karl Barth captured the spirit of the *kairos* moment when he said, "On Sunday morning when the bells ring to call the congregation and minister to worship, there is in the air an expectancy that something great, crucial, and momentous is to happen . . . . 'God is present! God *is* present.'"[1]

The meaning of the Greek word *kairos* will help us understand better what Barth was saying. The Greek language has a variety of terms to express the experience of time. One is *chronos*, which refers to a linear period of time. When time is thought of as a point or moment, the favored Greek word is *kairos*. The *kairos* moment is the right moment, the favorable opportunity, the time for making the crucial decision.

Kairos is the "today" of the gospel call. I read once of a homiletics teacher who claimed the purpose of preaching is to "raise the dead." That definition may be a bit unsophisticated, but it makes a vital point. It is during the *kairos* preaching moment that God seeks to enter the private, no-trespassing areas of our lives, those areas where our comfort zones may be disturbed and our "little sins" put under God's microscope—but also where our wounds may be healed.

The stakes are high in preaching. Who but God can know how He intends to fulfill His purposes through the spoken Word? What happens in preaching radiates throughout the Church's life and mission. Congregations not only want to hear well-executed preaching, they urgently need it to experience the transforming power of God's Word preached.

THE PREDICAMENT

Preaching has fallen upon hard times in many Protestant churches. Critics of preaching have doubted its effectiveness in our modern television-oriented generation. Even the pastor may question the value of devoting a major segment of time to sermon preparation. As well, the pastor's own congregation may not appreciate the time and effort good preaching demands. However, the preacher needs to remember what every preacher knows, that Protestant congregations in general continue to rate preaching at the top of the pastor's various duties and the sermon as the most important part of the worship service.

Another modern challenge to solid biblical preaching is the increased use of sociology and psychology in preaching. William Willimon claims the two fundamental weaknesses of contemporary Protestant preaching are "moralizing" and "psychologizing."[2] Willimon defines moralizing as offering the gospel in the form of suggestions for better living, principles for correct opinion, or obligations to be met. Psychologizing occurs when the preacher invokes a psychologically-oriented set of principles, programs, or advice designed to help the listener feel better, and/or to enable him or her to deal more adequately with the challenges of everyday life.

No doubt both "moralizing" and "psychologizing" are needed in society. However, preaching may not be the place for them. Both tend too easily toward a kind of naturalism operating mainly on the human level. Good advice and moral instruction alone stop short of the supernatural transforming grace of God. At the center of the preaching moment must be the Christ of God, presented to the listener as the grace of God.

Another issue contributing to the preaching moment predicament is raised by the lack of interest in setting off Sunday as a "church day." The centrality of the Sunday preaching event is obscured in many churches by the "full-program church" mentality, overshadowed by an ever-increasing complex of church activities. Sunday school classes, youth meetings, weekly Bible studies, and many other worthwhile programs *can* cause the American pragmatic, work-oriented society to view the time spent in the worship hour as a non-productive period. The preacher will do well, then, to find ways to elevate and emphasize the centrality of weekly worship as a time when the Holy Spirit works to transform the lives of listeners through the power of the preached Word of God.

THE PARISHIONERS

The church is first called to *be* rather than to *do*. Roman Catholic scholar Bernard Cooke underscores this point in *Ministry to Word and Sacraments*. After surveying the various ministries of the church he concludes, "Yet one cannot avoid the impression that the principal ministry of the community is exercised by being a community of faith and love, and as such, bearing witness to the presence of God's saving action in Christ and the Spirit."[3]

The worship service is a vital part of the preaching moment. How often has a family gathered—despondent, overwhelmed, hopeless, and confused—to join God's people in worship, only to leave as new people? How many times has a weak, despondent, anguished soul emerged from the worship hour heartened to trust Christ despite difficult circumstances? Indeed, in worship and the preaching of the Word we meet and are met by God.

> The greatest preachers have always been lovers of the Bible.
>
> —John Killinger,
> *Fundamentals of Preaching*

The Spirit-sanctioned experience of corporate worship mandates that the preacher and congregation alike catch a glimpse of the New Testament church. When the church is indeed the church, the atmosphere of God's presence opens the soul to the searching work of the Holy Spirit. When God's felt presence saturates the soil of corporate worship, even unbelievers are drawn to Christ.

Thus, the Holy Spirit must be free to work in the worship service. It is true that the Spirit can work in any way and at any time He pleases. However, God invites us to partner with Him in winning and discipling the world. One way that can happen is for people to be moved to commit themselves to God under our preaching. It follows, then, that our best preparation for worship is required.

> The power of a disciplined spiritual life radiates out into all the other areas of a minister's existence.
>
> —Phillips Brooks, *Lectures on Preaching*

Besides the obvious need for the preacher's sermon preparation, let me suggest two different commitments to prayer as important worship preparation. First, prayer should be a central part of our planning for the worship service. The content of the worship service should, in the main, point to the sermon, and the sermon ought to be the focal point of the worship service. If the whole is to point the congregation to God, the planning of the whole must be bathed in prayer. Second, prayer is crucial to the worship hour itself. The preaching moment needs to be immersed in prayer. Wesley himself said that one is not saved unless they have prayed.

In my Michigan pastorate I promoted an early morning Sunday prayer meeting. In the middle of January, a 6:00 a.m. prayer meeting loses some of its appeal. Nevertheless, in that church Amos Keefer was one of the six or eight men who attended faithfully. Amos always prayed fervently that God would anoint the pastor and the sermon. A few hours later, I would feel the Holy Spirit honoring his prayer as I stood to preach. A real work of God's grace is made possible through prayer. The pastor is well advised to find people who will pray for the worship hour as well as for the pastor in the preaching moment.

PARTAKING OF DIVINE HOLINESS

Dennis Kinlaw, one of this generation's great holiness preachers, has written, "Ultimately there is no great preaching unless the preacher partakes of the divine holiness in some measure."[4] An unrelenting inclination can torment the pastor to allow the work of ministry to overshadow a personal walk with Christ. If a sense of Christ's presence is lost in the demands of our work, the joy and excitement of the ministry is lost with it. Our personal walk with Christ is vital to being a partaker of the divine holiness. James McCutcheon emphasizes the absolute necessity of prayer and Bible study to this end, noting they must be at the center because the preacher's disciplined spiritual life radiates out into all other areas of a minister's life.[5]

The preacher ought to pray for and expect the anointing of the Holy Spirit. I first heard the term "anointing" after I was converted out of a good but pagan home at the age of fifteen. Thus, as a young new convert, I was not familiar with the lingo of the church, but one statement I heard often was, "The pastor preached under the anointing." Even at my young age, though I did not fully understand the implications of that phrase, I knew it had something to do with the presence of God attending the preaching of the sermon.

It has been many years since I heard anyone speak of God's anointing on the preacher. Therefore, I was delighted to find it discussed in Donald Demaray's book, *Introduction to Homiletics*. In fact, in my review of some fifty homiletics books, Demaray was the only one to address the idea that "God Anoints the Preacher."[6] First, he points to God's anointing of Old Testament kings and prophets. Then he observes that Jesus himself engaged in ministry only after the Holy Spirit anointed Him at His baptism. At Nazareth Jesus linked this anointing to His future ministry

> True preaching is an event—an event that effectively communicates the power and redemptive activity of God.
>
> —John A. Broadus,
> *On the Preparation and Delivery of Sermons*

when He said, "The Spirit of the Lord is upon me, because he has anointed me to proclaim good news to the poor" (Luke 4:18).

W. E. Sangster's son Paul spoke of his father's anointing by the Holy Spirit. According to the younger Sangster, his father struggled in prayer over his desire for reputation and academic degrees and confessed, "I wanted degrees more than knowledge, and praise rather than equipment for service." Demaray offered this insightful conclusion, "Herein lies the secret of power in preaching. Without surrender and anointing, the preacher's words lack thrust and penetration."[7]

The Spirit's anointing is indefinable. Just as describing the color yellow cannot be done, so the embrace of the Holy Spirit with the warm fires and fresh breezes of His presence cannot easily be described. Yet it is real, and often it is felt.

PREACHING FOR A VERDICT

The sermon is an unrepeatable adventure. It is preached to and at the center of the community of faith. The preacher must never relinquish the conviction that the sermon has a unique power as it is preached to that community. Something happens then that can happen only in, by, and through the sermon. The preacher, therefore, must have an absolute conviction that God speaks powerfully through the preached Word.

Recently, Bailey, and Wiersbe asked, "What about the idea of 'preaching for a verdict'? Is that still valid today?"[8] Wiersbe then made a startling observation, "Many churches no longer give invitations for the lost to come and trust Christ."[9] Why, after pouring out his or her heart for thirty minutes, would the preacher fail to give people an opportunity for a personal response?

WE OR YOU?

Preaching for a verdict is essential to the preaching moment, so the sermon must be direct and personal. Have you noticed how often, when a restaurant server walks up to a table to take an order, the question is, "Are we ready to order yet?" The preacher often has the same tendency to avoid the second person "you." But, clearly, the use of the second person properly conveys more power. "We" weakens the message.

In my younger days my father taught me to hunt. Early on, I learned the difference between a rifle and shotgun. Whereas a shotgun fires a load of small pellets, a rifle fires a single bullet. In like fashion, the preacher's sermon should be aimed at the hearer's heart with all the precision of a sharp-shooting rifleman. "We" is the shotgun; "you" is the rifle.

> Despite all the evidence to the contrary—people both need and want the Word of God.
>
> —W. E. Sangster, *The Craft of Sermon Construction*

Dr. Earle Wilson relates an occasion when a pastor asked him to evaluate his preaching. Dr. Wilson had found the sermon to be well constructed and delivered, but it had achieved little recognizable result. He observed, "To preach a sermon worth listening to requires a great deal of preparation time in the study, prayer in the closet, personal commitment to the truth being delivered; and spiritual, emotional, and even physical energy. No preacher wants such commitment to become just an exercise in futility." Speaking of the hearers, Dr. Wilson continued, "People need to be inspired to live on with hope; convicted to repent and change their ways; and to be instructed in the thoughts of God until God's thoughts become their thoughts. When preaching for a verdict the preacher must speak into reality words of meaning that people can open their hearts to and be changed by!"[10]

A PASSION FOR TRUTH AND LIFE

Preaching for a verdict demands belief in the biblical themes of sin, guilt, and salvation. Preaching for a verdict requires the preacher's belief that in Christ Jesus the sin-sick soul can find grace, forgiveness, and restoration. Preaching for a verdict is not possible if the sermon's major theme is the recipe for good mental health rather than the Holy Spirit's power to enter human personality with the purpose of making the believer more like Jesus.

> God fully expects the church of Jesus Christ to prove itself a miraculous group in the midst of a hostile world.
>
> —A. W. Tozer, *I Call It Heresy!*

Samuel Beckett's famous play, *Waiting for Godot*, focuses on the author's observations of the absurdity of life. In the play, two tramps named Didi and Gogo engage in a meaningless conversation. Didi and Gogo were captivated by Lucky, another character in the play, who could mumble philosophical phrases by putting a hat on his head. While wearing the hat, Lucky quoted phrases from great philosophers of the Western world, but the quotations and his thoughts had neither coherence nor cohesion.

Any preacher who is like Lucky will never be able to preach for a verdict. Sermon preparation characterized by carelessly and thoughtlessly hooking together a few sentences from the Internet, or even from *The Complete Works of John Wesley*, will never reach the hearts of listeners. Preaching for a verdict must speak to human hurts and hopes, to real life needs and aspirations. Genuine preaching develops partly out of the hospital room, the counseling session, and the casual daily encounters with folks in the marketplaces of life.

When the preacher preaches for a verdict, the text of the sermon must evoke thoughts, feelings, and convictions in the preacher. Recently a student shared with me about a sermon she intended to preach in her homiletics class. She said that during the day's activities the sermon traveled up and down the hallways of her heart and mind; she had even been dreaming about it. That kind of sermon saturation is essential to preaching for a verdict. It was no surprise that she won the award for the best sermon manuscript in her homiletics class.

Preaching that searches the souls of listeners is an extraordinary phenomenon. Preaching for a verdict involves what Sangster calls a "terrible personalness."[11] Where else does an individual stand before a congregation of listeners, to probe, provoke, and pierce the hearts and minds of others?

IS THERE ANY WORD?

The effectiveness of what the preacher says depends in large measure on how it is said. We need to communicate that something vital is at stake, to speak with urgency and intensity, to prove that the audible voice of God's call to His people is not dull, dead, or dry as dust. Human hurt and godly grace may be written in the sermon manuscript; but unless we enter empathically into the real-life situations of our people, our thoughts are leaden, and the best sermon content becomes abstract and irrelevant. The voice of the preacher is crucial in preaching for a verdict.

John Killinger reminds us that when sailing ships were the only means of communication from the old countries, people in America anxious for news from relatives and loved ones would gather at the dock as soon as a mast was

> The greatest essential in connection with preaching is the unction and the anointing of the Holy Spirit.
>
> —D. Martyn Lloyd-Jones, *Preaching and Preachers*

sighted. The moment the gangplank was lowered, the sailors were asked by the anxious crowd, "Is there any word?" and, again, "Is there any word?"

In a world of electronic gadgetry, modern men and women who feel alienated and cut off from community put the same question to the preacher, "Is there any word?" This knowledge frees the preacher, indeed impels us, to call for a verdict. The saving word comes from the Bible that speaks directly and authoritatively to people's needs.

The preaching moment is uniquely unrepeatable. The sermon can be preserved in print, but it cannot be frozen in time. Those in attendance experience a *kairos* moment; some may never experience another. The preacher *must* seize that moment, and preach for a verdict. Eternal destinies depend on it.

ACTION SUGGESTIONS

1. Establish how the components of the worship service will contribute to the objectives of the sermon. Plan the worship around the sermon's theme.

2. Strive to preach in the concrete. Preaching must be imagistic rather than abstract. Think about how the imagery of the sermon progresses toward clarifying the verdict. In other words, how do the illustrations of the sermon lead the listener to the sermon's verdict objective? For example, Jesus' parables were imagistic, and they aimed at a singular response. When asked, "Who is my neighbor?" Jesus made the answer crystal clear in the parable of the Good Samaritan.

3. Consider these and similar questions as you strive to develop your preaching for a verdict: How was the claim of God upon the listeners developed in the sermon? Were the conditions of the claim clear or indefinite? Make sure your preaching of God's claim displays urgency and intensity that leads listeners to realize something is at stake.

4. Practice moving from the first person plural "we" to the second person singular "you." Dr. Earle Wilson rightly suggests, "Early in the message the preacher should use plural pronouns. The sentences will be something like this; 'Let us consider this thought together.' As the sermon moves toward the conclusion the sentences should sound like this, 'Do you realize that unless you repent you will be lost?'"

FOR FURTHER READING

Brooks, Phillips. *Lectures on Preaching*. Grand Rapids: Zondervan Publishing House, 1984 [1877].

A compilation of the great New England preacher's Lyman Beecher Lectures of 1877, this volume stands as one of the most inspiring books on preaching ever written, putting strong emphasis on the relationship of the pastor to preaching. (It has been republished recently under the title, *The Joy of Preaching*.)

Fant, Clyde E. *Preaching for Today*. San Francisco: Harper & Row, 1987.

Fant focuses on what preaching can do. His conclusion is that "preaching can send the church into the real world."

Kinlaw, Dennis F. *Preaching in the Spirit*. Grand Rapids: Francis Asbury Press, 1985.

Kinlaw addresses several homiletical issues, but his main focus is on the dynamic influence of the Holy Spirit upon the preaching event.

Long, Thomas G. *The Senses of Preaching*. Atlanta, John Knox Press, 1988.

Long investigates four aspects of preaching which, taken together, provide an analysis of the congregation/preacher relationships.

Lueking, Dean F. *Preaching: The Art of Connecting God and People*. Waco: Word Books, 1985.

Lueking contends that people contribute to great preaching in more ways than one. His purpose is to show how to "incorporate people into the preached Word, to give a voice to the hopes and fears, the victories and defeats, that are a part of the journey of faith."

NOTES

1. Karl Barth, *The Word of God and the Word of Man* (New York: Harper & Row, 1928), 104.

2. William Willimon and Robert L. Wilson, *Preaching and Worship in the Small Church* (Nashville: Abingdon Press, 1980), 104–5.

3. Bernard Cooke, *Ministry to Word and Sacrament* (Minneapolis: Augsburg Fortress Press, 1980), 183.

4. Dennis F. Kinlaw, *Preaching in the Spirit* (Grand Rapids: Francis Asbury Press, 1985), 18.

5. James McCutcheon, *The Pastoral Ministry* (Nashville: Abingdon Press, 1978), 17.

6. Donald E. Demaray, *Introduction to Homiletics* (Indianapolis: Light and Life Press, 1990), 27.

7. Ibid., 28–29.

8. E. K. Bailey and Warren W. Wiersbe, *Preaching in Black and White* (Grand Rapids: Zondervan, 2003), 119ff.

9. Ibid.

10. Conversation with author in May 2005.

11. W. E. Sangster, *The Craft of Sermon Construction* (Grand Rapids: Baker Book House, 1972), 25.

AFTERWORD

Aspiring to Be an Effective Preacher

When a person responds to the call of God to preach the gospel that person is immediately thrust into a fascinating world of great and gifted personalities. Perhaps in no other profession are we so privileged to "tread where the saints have trod." What could be a more thrilling life adventure than to journey with Chalmers, Spurgeon, Wesley, Whitfield, Jonathan Edwards, D. L. Moody, Billy Sunday, and Billy Graham? The preacher's life is immeasurably rewarding. It is also almost unbearably demanding.

THE MARK OF GREAT PREACHERS

It is interesting that no art form allows for such diversity of style as does preaching. In fact, it is not easy to determine why one person becomes a great preacher and another does not. Two people may appear to have equal gifts; they may even attend the same school and both be graduated with honors. Yet, one may become a preacher whom the world will never forget while the other is soon forgotten. More than that, the Christian pulpit has had many an Abraham Lincoln—obscure at the start, self-educated, arising to world fame. Gipsy Smith preached to some of the largest congregations ever gathered. He began life as a nomad, without a country or a nationality; yet when he died in 1947, at the age of eighty-seven, five countries were eager to claim him as their own. While oratory attracts the multitudes, many have been noted orators and yet poor preachers.

Determining those characteristics upon which a preacher's greatness depends is difficult. Superficial people are inclined to test a preacher's greatness by one's popularity or by the fact that he or she is an orator. Learned people will inquire whether the preacher is an original thinker. Every person will have his or her own answer to the question; all will have their own tests of greatness.

Many great preachers have been outstanding Bible expositors. Still others have been reformers who have cried out prophet-like against the abuses of their day. Another class of great preachers have been evangelists. The names of Whitefield and Wesley are preeminent among them, for these fearless men and their associates led their vast outdoor congregations to Mount Sinai; and when the thunderings of the Law terrified them, they were led to Mount Calvary and to the Cross.

The reputation of other preachers rests upon the fact that they were outstanding teachers. Charles Simeon of Cambridge influenced many people; so did Robertson of Brighton. Eccentric old John Duncan, of New College, Edinburgh, commonly known to his students as "Rabbi" Duncan because he taught Hebrew, exerted a powerful influence upon the pulpits of Scotland.

A class of preachers often overlooked are the missionaries and the pioneers. These may not have attracted great congregations, but their splendid achievements in distant lands brought them lasting luster. One might mention William Carey, Henry Martyn, David Livingstone, Robert Moffat, and a long list of others, not forgetting the pioneer preachers who went to the American colonies and did much to establish Christianity in a new land.

In judging the excellence of a preacher, such things as eloquence, personality, and outward success are not necessarily the final test. Jonathan Edwards was a quiet man, he read his sermons closely, he made no attempt at oratory, and after a few years his congregation asked him to resign; yet several whose opinions are authoritative assure us that Edwards was the greatest preacher America has produced. One must consider things other than oratory, personality, and material success in estimating the enduring greatness of a preacher.

While it is no easy task to determine just what elements enter into a preacher's greatness, there are some constants. A note of urgency and a gift of persuasiveness are important qualities of all great preachers; without these, eloquence and literary style count for little. Great preachers have the ability to present evangelical truth clearly and without fear; without something valuable to say, persuasion leads nowhere.

A simple shepherd lad, spelling his way through a Greek Testament which he had walked forty-eight miles to buy, became the great John Brown of Haddington, Bible scholar and preacher of sin and grace.

GREAT PREACHERS TODAY

How many men and women aspire to greatness in preaching today? In a day of church builders, technicians, and worship gurus, is there a place for strong preaching from influential pulpits—preaching which rises above the level of mediocrity and will leave behind a legacy of transformation and reformation? Effective preaching must make people realize their sinfulness by nature, their need of repentance, the futility of their unaided efforts to better themselves spiritually, the need of a Savior, and the power of the Grace of God in Jesus Christ our Lord. No preacher is truly great unless he or she can convince the listeners of the hideousness of sin, of the need of implicit faith in the righteousness and blood of Jesus Christ, and of the reality of the benefits of His atoning work received through the power of the Holy Spirit evidenced through divinely appointed means. The preacher who is able to do this is an evangelical preacher, and that person's labors will bear fruit in the form of changed lives.

In the truest sense of the word, we have not chosen the ministry as a profession; God has chosen us. True, many facets and features of ministry today lie far beyond the preaching function. It also remains true, however, that if we would influence people, change a culture for the better, reinforce biblical standards of morality and ethics, and leave a legacy that will truly outlive us, we must give ourselves to the study of the Word of God and to a commitment to communicate that Word clearly, passionately, persuasively, and powerfully. To do that, we need to learn from the masters of preaching.

It still remains true that, ultimately, the greatest problems facing our society are spiritual problems. People simply are in need of God in their lives, whether they know it or not. To paraphrase Romans 10:14–17, "They will not ask for help unless they believe in Him, and they will not believe in Him unless they have heard of Him, and they will not hear of Him unless they get a preacher, and they will never have a preacher unless one is sent. But as the Scripture says, the footsteps of those who bring good news is a welcome sound. . . . So faith comes from what is preached, and what is preached comes from the Word of Christ."

This book is written for you. It is designed to inspire and assist you in taking the preaching ministry seriously. Take advantage of what these gifted writers have placed in your hands. They will inspire you to be a better preacher than you ever thought you could be. Having digested what is here, go out to your world with a greater desire to preach the Word to dying people, bringing hope and eternal life to all who will listen and obey.

—Earle L. Wilson

ABOUT
THE AUTHORS

GARETH LEE COCKERILL was ordained a minister in The Wesleyan Church in 1969; he is a member of the Shenandoah District. Dr. Cockerill is Professor of New Testament and Biblical Theology at Wesley Biblical Seminary, Jackson, Mississippi. He earned the B.A. degree from Southern Wesleyan University, the M.Div. from Asbury Theological Seminary, and the Th.M. and Ph.D. degrees from Union Theological Seminary in Virginia. Dr. Cockerill is currently writing a commentary on Hebrews to be published by Eerdman's in the New International Commentary on the New Testament series.

Dr. Cockerill and his wife Rosa served for nine years as missionaries in Sierra Leone, West Africa, where they were engaged in evangelism, teaching, administration, and medical ministries. The Cockerills have three adult daughters, one son-in-law, and one grandson.

JOSEPH E. COLESON was ordained in the Northwest District of The Wesleyan Church in 1979. His B.A. is from Indiana Wesleyan University, his M.A. and Ph.D. degrees from Brandeis University. He has been Professor of Old Testament at Nazarene Theological Seminary since 1995; previously, he was on the faculties of Roberts Wesleyan College, Rochester, New York, and Western Evangelical Seminary, Portland, Oregon. Dr. Coleson's pastoral experience is in four congregations of the United

Methodist Church in the Western New York and Missouri Conferences.

Dr. Coleson currently is working on Joshua for the Tyndale House New Living Translation commentary series and on Genesis for a commentary series newly launched by Nazarene Publishing House. He enjoys family life with his wife, Charlotte, their two grown children and spouses, and two grandchildren. Traveling to teach, reading mystery novels, and gardening are other interests.

JOSEPH R. DONGELL is an ordained minister in The Wesleyan Church, having been ordained in the South Carolina District. Dr. Dongell is Professor of Biblical Studies at Asbury Theological Seminary, Wilmore, Kentucky. He holds the B.A. degree from Southern Wesleyan University, the M.Div. from Asbury Theological Seminary, the M.A. from the University of Kentucky, and the Ph.D. from Union Theological Seminary in Virginia. Dr. Dongell's scholarly interests include Lukan Studies, Pauline Theology, and New Testament Greek.

Joseph is the husband of Regina, and father of Jordan and Janna. He is trying his best to be a better gardener.

DAVID E. EATON was ordained in the California District of The Wesleyan Church in 1962. Dr. Eaton earned the B.A. degree from Azusa Pacific University, the M.A. from Pasadena College, and the M. Phil. and Ph.D. degrees from Drew University. He is Professor and Chair of the Division of Religion and Philosophy at Oklahoma Wesleyan University, where he has taught for the past twenty years. Prior to his teaching career at OWU, he served as senior pastor of several significant congregations in The Wesleyan Church.

Dr. Eaton collects ceramic and wood artworks; his collection includes several ceramic replicas of birds inscribed on Pennsylvania birth certificates. He also has several bird houses and feeders in his back yard, and several birds "which enjoy a great life in the Eaton home."

RICHARD ECKLEY is an ordained minister in The Wesleyan Church and Associate Professor of Theology at Houghton College. He also serves parttime as Assistant to the Pastor of The Wesleyan Church of Orchard Park, New York. Dr. Eckley holds the B.S. degree from United Wesleyan College, the M.Div. from Asbury Theological Seminary, and the Th.M. from Princeton Theological Seminary. His Ph.D. from Duquesne University was a study of pneumatology in current ecumenical theology.

Rich and his wife Lynn recently have taken to scuba diving to get as deep into the world as possible.

CARLTON FISHER was raised in The Wesleyan Church in Ohio and Indiana and graduated from Indiana Wesleyan University with a B.A. degree; he also holds an M.A. from Western Kentucky University. After earning an M.A. and a Ph.D. from Notre Dame and pastoring briefly in the Indiana North District of The Wesleyan Church, he joined the faculty of Houghton College in 1985; he teaches philosophy and serves in academic administration.

Carlton and his wife, Joyce, have two sons and a daughter-in-law.

JO ANNE LYON was ordained in the Tri-State District of The Wesleyan Church in 1996. She earned her Bachelor's degree at the University of Cincinnati and her Master's at the University of Missouri, Kansas City. She did further work in Theology at Saint Louis University, and holds several honorary degrees, as well. Dr. Lyon is best known as the founder of World Hope, International, a relief and aid agency. From establishing medical clinics to distributing international aid funds, she has led World Hope to become a diversified organization meeting the needs of others and empowering them to achieve a better life. Dr. Lyon has been recognized as an "agent of peace and reconciliation," and a change agent in the United States and many other countries.

Dr. Lyon has been involved in pastoral ministry in the local church setting, both inner-city and suburban. She preaches on college campuses, at retreats, in revival services, and in multi-denominational conventions. She preaches internationally, as well, in Africa, Asia, Europe, Australia, and Latin America.

Dr. Lyon enjoys playing softball with her four grandchildren and discovering out-of-the-way "greasy spoon" restaurants with her husband.

BILL PEED was ordained in the South Carolina District of The Wesleyan Church in 1979. He earned the B.S. degree from Clemson University, the M.A. from Wheaton College, and the Ph.D. from Trinity Evangelical Divinity School. Dr. Peed and his wife Marilee served with Global Partners, the international missions arm of The Wesleyan Church, as career missionaries to Zambia, where Bill's interests in cross-cultural communications and ministry effectiveness were deepened. Research for his Ph.D. dissertation focused on the intercultural competencies of Wesleyan missionaries.

Dr. Peed is the Global Ministry Program Director at Bethany Bible College, Sussex, New Brunswick, Canada, where he has served since 2003. The Peeds have been married for thirty years; they have three children.

KEN SCHENCK is Associate Professor of Religion at Indiana Wesleyan University where he has been a member of the faculty since 1997. He earned the A.B. degree from Southern Wesleyan University, the M.Div. from Asbury Theological Seminary, the M.A.

from the University of Kentucky, and the Ph.D. from the University of Durham, England.

Dr. Schenck was ordained a minister in the Wesleyan Church in the Florida District in 1991. He is married to Angela; they have three daughters and a son. His recent and current work includes *Understanding the Book of Hebrews* and *A Brief Guide to Philo*, both from Westminster John Knox Press; *Jesus is Lord: An Introduction to the New Testament*, from IWU's Triangle Publishing; and *1 and 2 Corinthians*, from Wesleyan Publishing House. He says that when "deadlines aren't suffocating" him, he likes to jog.

PAUL W. SHEA, Assistant Professor of Missions at Houghton College, has served The Wesleyan Church as an ordained minister for thirty-three years, having been ordained in 1973 by the Illinois District. He has served for five years as a pastor in the United States, twelve years as a missionary in Sierra Leone, West Africa, and fifteen years as an educator. Dr. Shea earned the B.A. degree from Houghton College, the M.Div. and D. Miss. degrees from Trinity Evangelical Divinity School.

Paul's parents, Alton and Aileen Shea, ignited his interest in Christ, the church, and missions by humbly modeling Christ-like, compassionate living and good preaching—Dad from the pulpit and Mom with powerful weekly children's sermons. All three of his own daughters have spent significant time in Africa as adults, in teaching, nursing, and research; they "caught the Africa bug as MKs." By the way, Paul recently handed in his basketball sneakers for a pair of golf shoes.

R. DUANE THOMPSON, Ph.D., was ordained by the Indiana North District of The Wesleyan Church in 1954. He earned a Ph.D. in Philosophy from Boston University in 1962, with a dissertation titled, *Maritain and Tillich: Art and Religion*. He is Professor Emeritus from Indiana Wesleyan University where he was Chair of the Division of Religion and Philosophy for seventeen years.

Dr. Thompson enjoys travel at home and abroad. He is "especially delighted with family involvements," his wife, their children, and their grandchildren. He also is an avid reader.

R. DUANE THOMPSON II is pastor of First United Methodist Church in Washington, Pennsylvania. He is an Elder and Member of the Western Pennsylvania Conference of the United Methodist Church, having been ordained in 1996. Dr. Thompson earned the B.A. degree from Miami University, Oxford, Ohio, the J.D. from the George Washington University National Law Center, and the M.Div. from Union Theological Seminary, New York. All the churches he has served have seen significant growth under his leadership. He recently received a Sabbatical Grant for Pastoral Leaders from the Louisville Institute to study the theme "Contemplating and Communicating Forgiveness."

Dr. Thompson is married to Brenda; their interests include travel, especially through England, Scotland, and other parts of Europe; reading, especially literature and history; and physical fitness.

J. MICHAEL WALTERS is Professor of Christian Ministries, and Chair of the Department of Religion and Philosophy at Houghton College. He is also Director of Ministerial Education at Houghton where he teaches preaching and advises ministerial students. He earned a B.A. degree from Circleville Bible College, a B.A. from Houghton College, an M.A.R. from Asbury Theological Seminary, an M.A. from St. Mary's University, and the D. Min. from Trinity Evangelical Divinity School.

Dr. Walters is an ordained minister in The Wesleyan Church, and spent eighteen years in pastoral ministry, including thirteen years as Senior Pastor to the Houghton College campus and the community of Houghton, New York, before joining the faculty of Houghton College. He loves almost all things Australian and is learning to play the didgeridoo.